COOK-OFF AMERICA

MAJOR FUNDING PROVIDED BY:

ADDITIONAL FUNDING PROVIDED BY:

Prize-Winning Recipes from the Public Television Series

COOK-OFF AMERICA

Produced by Marjorie Poore Productions

Food Photography by Darla Furlani
Location Photograhy by Alec Fatalevich

TABLE OF CONTENTS

INTRODUCTION

COOK-OFF AMERICA may never have happened if it weren't for my friend, Jim Heywood. By day Jim is a mild-mannered instructor at the prestigious and pristine Culinary Institute of America. Come the weekend, Jim sheds his white chef's coat, slips into blue jeans, replaces his chef toque with a cowboy hat and is ready to assume his second identity as a "chili-head". It was Jim who encouraged me to investigate the chili competitions. I was immediately enamored by the wonderful world of cook-offs and food festivals where you can find some of the best regional cooking this country has to offer. From the salmon in Eastport, Maine to the barbecue in Memphis, Tennessee to the garlic in Gilroy, California—everywhere we went we discovered wonderful local specialties and prize-winning recipes. In addition, we found endless enthusiasm and community spirit among the people who planned the festivals, as well as the competitors who cooked the food.

IT TOOK US OVER A YEAR to cover all the various events for our first season of Cook-Off America. Our first stop was in Reno, Nevada, for the International Chili Society's World Championship Chili Cook-Off. I had heard about chili fanatics, but it wasn't until the end of our two-day stay with thousands of chili-heads that I really began to understand the passion that chili can generate. Our next stop was Orlando, Florida, for the Mama Mary's Gourmet Pizza Crusts Pizza Creations Contest. It was here that I had my first encounter with "contesters" as they call them on the circuit—people who enter contests as a hobby. Most of them are incredibly talented cooks who instinctively understand how ingredients come together.

And while many of them are capable of writing cookbooks, most prefer to remain amateur regulars on the cook-off circuit.

OUR NEXT ADVENTURE was in Boulder, Colorado, in the dead of winter for the National Pie Championships. Initially, I found the lack of oxygen in the area somewhat debilitating, but even in my listless state, I managed to muster up the strength to sample a healthy number of the more than 400 pies available for tasting. When we weren't eating our way through the flaky pie crusts and luscious fillings, we were viewing the pie art, listening to the poetry readings, and watching the pie making classes for kids.

JUST AS SPRING STARTED TO BREAK, we ventured to the Vidalia Onion Festival in Vidalia, Georgia, where I rediscovered onion rings (albeit a heavenly new breed that can't compare to what you find in fast food chains). We visited a charming family of onion growers, the Stanleys, who graciously let us tour and film their fields. The Stanleys sent us home with Vidalia onion relish, Vidalia onion salsa, Vidalia onion pickles, and of course, Vidalia onions, 40 pounds' worth, which my husband hand-carried on the plane trip home.

BY LATE SPRING, it was time for one of the greatest festivals of all—Memphis in May. Despite the warnings, I was not prepared for the Mardi Gras-like atmosphere that takes over this little spot of barbecue heaven along the Mississippi River. It was in Memphis that I discovered that I had been deprived of really good barbecue for most of my life. Of course, I tried to make up by sampling as much as I could. As a bonus, we met Memphis' barbecue king, John Willingham, owner of Willingham's World Champion BBQ Restaurant, whose devotion to barbecue is inspirational.

BY THE END OF MAY it was time for the Jambalaya Festival in Gonzales, Louisiana. Jambalaya has special meaning to the people of southern Louisiana who treasure their jambalaya recipes like family heirlooms. It's truly amazing how heated a competition can get even when every participant is using exactly the same ingredients! As July ended, we were back in our neck of the woods—Northern California—for the Gilroy Garlic Festival, an event that no food lover should miss. Over 125,000 people gather to eat foods drenched in garlic: shrimp scampi, calamari, French bread, stuffed mushrooms, pepper steak sandwiches, and for dessert, garlic ice cream. To pass the time in-between eating, there are cooking demonstrations, garlic-braiding contests, children's play activities, and three stages of live entertainment.

AS FALL APPROACHED, we noticed our schedule of food events getting tighter and tighter. We decided to head to the north of Maine for the Salmon Festival in Eastport, a quaint, old-fashioned New England village, and the Eastern-most city in the U.S. In Eastport, salmon farming has breathed new life into a dying sardine fishing area. After dining on barbecued salmon burgers, it was down to Kennett Square, Pennsylvania, an area that produces 25 percent of U.S. mushrooms. Its annual Mushroom Festival and cook-off turns out sophisticated recipes prepared by challengers from all over the country.

IN EARLY OCTOBER we attended Sutter Home Winery's Build a Better Burger Contest which takes place in Napa Valley, California. We witnessed the building of some pretty phenomenal and imaginative burgers. From Napa, it was on to another Northern California city, Half Moon Bay, the pumpkin capital of the world, which hosts a terrific pumpkin festival every year. The fun starts with a pumpkin weigh-in (this year's largest weighed 972 pounds) and continues with pumpkin pie-eating contests, pumpkin carving sessions, and more. As Thanksgiving approached, so did the Massachusetts Cranberry Harvest Festival, held at a cranberry bog in South Carver. The cranberry farmers have a lot to celebrate with cranberries' tremendous growth in popularity in the last ten years.

AFTER SLOSHING THROUGH CRANBERRY BOGS and pumpkin fields, we cleaned ourselves up to attend the Newman's Own and Good Housekeeping Recipe Contest, held at the Rainbow Room in New York City. The elegance of the room did not stop the judges (Paul Newman, Joanne Woodward, their daughter Nell Newman and actress Glenn Close) from exhibiting genuine excitement for the winning recipes. We ended our tour with a step back in time at the Henry Ford Museum in Dearborn, Michigan, which has done a magnificent job preserving the kitchens and cooking traditions or our past. For our visit, the museum staged authentic Christmas celebrations in several of their historic homes.

ALONG OUR JOURNEY we collected the wonderful recipes that appear in this book and witnessed first hand the pride and love from which these dishes originate. Each dish carries a memory of a different part of our country, and demonstrates a way of cooking that has its own unique style and appeal. We're proud to assemble them here for you to enjoy at home.

—*Marjorie Poore*

FRENCH-STYLE CHICKEN WITH APPLES

Georgia Apple Festival

Courtesy of The U.S. Apple Association · This dish is reminiscent of those made in the Normandy region of France, which is famous for its apples and apple products.

6 boneless, skinless chicken breast halves

1 onion, sliced

6 to 8 artichoke hearts, cut in half

3 Empire apples, cored and sliced

3 tablespoons apple brandy, apple cider or apple juice

One 10-ounce can condensed chicken broth

Pinch of ground cinnamon

Pinch of ground nutmeg

Salt and freshly ground pepper to taste

Minced fresh dill or parsley for garnish

✪ Spray a large nonstick skillet with nonstick cooking spray and place over medium heat. Add the chicken breasts and brown on both sides; transfer to a plate.

✪ Add the onion, artichokes and apples to the skillet and sauté for 2 to 3 minutes.

✪ Return the chicken to the skillet. Add the apple brandy or juice, chicken broth, cinnamon and nutmeg.

✪ Reduce the heat to low and simmer, covered, for 10 to 15 minutes, until the chicken is tender and cooked through. Season with salt and pepper.

✪ To serve, place one chicken breast on each of 6 serving plates and spoon the apple and artichoke mixture over the top. Garnish with fresh dill or parsley.

SERVES 6

APPLE COLESLAW

Georgia Apple Festival

David Corley and James Crocker, Owners, The Elderberry Inn and Restaurant, Ellijay, Georgia · David and James developed this recipes to showcase the prized products grown in their home town, "the Apple Capital of Georgia." The recipe has become so popular at their restaurant, several large orders for the slaw are placed each week.

1 carrot, shredded

$1/3$ cup shredded purple cabbage

8 cups shredded green cabbage

2 medium to large apples of your choice, cored and cubed

$1/3$ cup thick mayonnaise

$2/3$ cup sugar

Salt and freshly ground pepper to taste

✪ In a large bowl, combine the carrot, purple cabbage, green cabbage, apples, mayonnaise, sugar, salt and pepper and toss together well.

✪ Cover the bowl and let stand for 30 minutes before serving.

SERVES 10 TO 12

CREAM CHEESE APPLE PIE

Georgia Apple Festival

First Place, Pie Category: Shelby Thomas, Calhutta, Georgia • Shelby takes the best elements of cheesecake and apple pie and combines them in one irresistible dessert.

Two 9-inch pie shells (unbaked)

One 8-ounce package cream cheese

1/2 cup caramel ice cream topping

1/2 cup sugar

2 tablespoons all-purpose flour

1 teaspoon ground cinnamon

1 teaspoon vanilla extract

1/8 teaspoon salt

1 egg

4 cups chopped Granny Smith or other tart apples

TOPPING

3/4 cup sugar

3/4 cup all-purpose flour

1/2 cup butter

3/4 cup chopped pecans

✪ Preheat the oven to 400 degrees.

✪ Line two 9-inch pie pans with the pie pastry.

✪ In a bowl, combine the cream cheese, caramel topping, sugar, flour, cinnamon, vanilla and salt and beat until a smooth batter is formed.

✪ Add the egg and beat until well mixed.

✪ Add the apples and stir with a wooden spoon until well mixed.

✪ Pour the mixture into the pastry-lined pans, dividing evenly.

✪ Bake the pies for 20 minutes. Reduce the oven heat to 350 degrees and bake for 10 minutes.

✪ While the pies are baking, make the topping: combine the sugar, flour and butter in a shallow bowl. With a pastry blender or two knives, cut the ingredients together until crumbly. Stir in the pecans.

✪ Sprinkle the topping evenly over the pies and continue to bake for 15 to 20 minutes, until golden; cool slightly.

✪ To serve, cut the pies into wedges.

MAKES TWO 9-INCH PIES

MISS LO'S HOLIDAY APPLE CAKE

Georgia Apple Festival

First Place, Cake Category: Lois Freeland, Powder Springs, Georgia · The apples not only add delicious flavor, but also impart a lovely moist quality to Lois's cake.

1½ cups vegetable oil

2 cups sugar

3 eggs

3 cups all-purpose flour

1 teaspoon salt

1 teaspoon baking soda

1 teaspoon ground cinnamon

3 cups diced, peeled red Delicious apples

1 cup walnuts, chopped

½ cup chopped fresh or canned cherries

✪ Preheat the oven to 350 degrees. Grease a tube or Bundt pan.

✪ In a large bowl, mix together the oil, sugar and eggs until well blended.

✪ In another bowl, mix together the flour, salt, baking soda and cinnamon until well blended.

✪ Add the flour mixture to the egg mixture and stir until the batter is well blended.

✪ Add the apples, walnuts and cherries and mix until the ingredients are evenly incorporated.

✪ Pour the mixture into the prepared pan and bake for about 1 hour and 15 minutes. Starting at 45 minutes, insert a toothpick into the center of the cake to check for doneness; the cake is done when the toothpick comes out clean.

SERVES 10 TO 12

STILTON AND TOASTED WALNUT BURGERS WITH GRILLED TOMATOES AND SPICY LEEKS

Sutter Home Winery Build a Better Burger Contest

Second Runner-Up: Theodore F. Skiba · For his burgers, Theodore uses Stilton, a creamy, pungent variety of blue cheese from England. If you wish, you can substitute another type of strong blue cheese, such as Gorgonzola or Roquefort.

4 tablespoons walnut oil

8 ounces walnuts, broken into coarse pieces

8 ounces Stilton cheese, crumbled

3 tablespoons butter

5 tablespoons canola oil

4 cups sliced leeks, white part only, 1/2-inch slices

2 cloves garlic, finely chopped

1 cup Sutter Home Chardonnay

2 teaspoons Paul Prudhomme's Vegetable Magic seasoning blend

Canola oil

2 large tomatoes, cut into 1/4-inch-thick slices

24 ounces ground sirloin

6 tablespoons good-quality port wine

Freshly ground black pepper to taste

Eight 1/2-inch-thick slices dense multigrain bread, toasted

2 cups coarsely chopped watercress

✪ Prepare a hot fire in a grill with a cover.

✪ In a large skillet, heat 2 tablespoons of the walnut oil over medium-low heat. Add the walnuts and cook, stirring constantly, for about 3 to 5 minutes, until golden brown. Cool. With a food processor, process 3/4 of the nuts until coarsely ground.

✪ Place the remaining walnuts in a small skillet. Add the Stilton and stir over low heat until the cheese melts. Set aside.

✪ In a large skillet, melt the butter over medium heat. Add the canola oil. Add the leeks and sauté over high heat for about 8 minutes, until they begin to brown. Add the garlic and cook for 1 minute. Remove the skillet from the heat and add the Chardonnay. Return the mixture to the heat and cook until all of the liquid has evaporated. Stir in the Vegetable Magic.

✪ Brush or wipe the grill with canola oil. Brush the tomatoes with canola oil and place them on the grill. Grill for 2 minutes on each side; set aside.

✪ In a bowl, combine the sirloin, reserved ground nuts and port wine; mix well with your hands. Divide the mixture into 4 portions and shape them into patties approximately the size of the bread.

✪ Brush the burgers with 1 tablespoon of the walnut oil and season with pepper. Grill the burgers for 4 minutes. Turn the patties over and top with the cheese-walnut mixture, dividing evenly. Close the grill cover and cook for 4 more minutes.

✪ To serve, top the bottom slices of bread with watercress, leeks, burgers and grilled tomatoes, in that order, dividing evenly. Brush the top bread slices with the remaining 1 tablespoon walnut oil and place on top of the burgers.

SERVES 4

CAROLINA PORK BARBECUE BURGERS

Sutter Home Winery Build a Better Burger Contest

Grand Prize: Larry Elder • Larry's burgers are fashioned after classic Carolina pork barbecue sandwiches, but since the meat is molded into patties instead of pulled into shreds, they're much easier to eat.

BARBECUE BURGER BALM

1/3 cup molasses

1/3 cup apple cider vinegar

1/4 cup spicy brown mustard

2 cloves garlic, minced

1/4 teaspoon cayenne pepper

Salt and freshly ground black pepper
   to taste

CAROLINA COLESLAW

3 cups finely shredded green cabbage

1/2 cup finely slivered red and/or green
   bell pepper

2 green onions, chopped

2 tablespoons mayonnaise

2 tablespoons Sutter Home Sauvignon
   Blanc

2 teaspoons sugar

Salt and freshly ground black pepper
   to taste

BURGERS

1 1/2 pounds ground pork

1 teaspoon Paul Prudhomme's Meat
   Magic seasoning blend

1/4 cup finely chopped red onion

4 seeded burger buns, split

✪ For the barbecue burger balm, combine all ingredients in a bowl and blend well.

✪ For the Carolina coleslaw, combine the cabbage, pepper and onions in a large bowl and toss until well mixed. In a small bowl, mix together the mayonnaise, wine, sugar, salt and pepper until well blended. Pour the mayonnaise mixture over the cabbage mixture and toss well. Cover and refrigerate.

✪ Prepare a medium-hot barbecue fire in a grill with a cover.

✪ For the burgers, combine the pork, Meat Magic blend, onion and 1/4 cup of the burger balm in a bowl. With your hands, mix the ingredients together, handling the mixture as little as possible to avoid compacting it too much. Divide the mixture into 4 equal portions and carefully form the portions into patties the size of the buns.

✪ Place the patties on the medium-hot grill, close the cover and cook for about 4 minutes, until the patties are browned on the bottom side. With a wide spatula, turn the patties over and baste with some of the burger balm. Cook for about 5 to 7 minutes, until the juices run clear when the patties are pierced. Continue basting as the patties are cooking.

✪ During the last few minutes of cooking, place the buns, cut-side down, on the outer edges of the grill rack and cook until lightly toasted.

✪ Place a patty on the bottom half of each bun. Top each patty with some of the Carolina coleslaw and cover with the top half of the buns.

SERVES 4

Caesar Salad & Flank Steak Burgers on Garlic Crostini

Sutter Home Winery Build a Better Burger Contest

First Prize: Jason R. Boulanger • Instead of a bun, Jason sandwiches his burgers between slices of grilled garlic bread. A mini Caesar salad stands in for the traditional lettuce, tomato and onion garnish.

BURGERS

1½ pounds ground flank steak

½ cup chopped fresh Italian parsley

2 medium shallots, minced

1 clove garlic, crushed

1 teaspoon salt, preferably Kosher

½ teaspoon lemon pepper seasoning

½ teaspoon cracked black pepper

3 tablespoons Sutter Home Zinfandel

DRESSING

2 tablespoons olive oil

2 tablespoons extra-virgin olive oil

1½ teaspoons red wine vinegar

¾ teaspoon balsamic vinegar

⅛ teaspoon salt, preferably kosher

3 anchovy fillets, chopped

2 cloves garlic, chopped

2 teaspoons lemon juice

¼ teaspoon chopped fresh Italian parsley

Olive oil for brushing

GARLIC CROSTINI

Eight ½-inch-thick slices sourdough bread

Extra-virgin olive oil

4 cloves garlic, cut in half

1½ cups shredded romaine lettuce

Shaved Parmesan cheese to taste

Parsley sprigs for garnish

✪ Prepare a medium-hot barbecue fire.

✪ For the burgers, combine all of the ingredients in a large bowl and mix with your hands. Divide the mixture into 4 equal portions and carefully form the portions into patties the size of the bread.

✪ For the dressing, combine the olive oils, vinegars and salt in a small jar with a lid; shake until well blended. Mash the anchovy fillets and garlic together on a cutting board until they form a paste; transfer the paste to a medium bowl. Add the oil-vinegar mixture to the bowl with the lemon juice and chopped parsley; whisk until the dressing is smooth and set aside.

✪ When the fire is ready, brush the grill rack with olive oil. Place the patties on the grill and cook them to the desired doneness: 3 to 4 minutes for medium-rare; 5 to 6 minutes for medium; and 8 to 9 minutes for well-done. Turn the patties once during cooking.

✪ For the crostini, brush the bread slices with the olive oil on both sides. During the last few minutes that the burgers are cooking, place the bread on the outer edges of the grill and cook until lightly toasted; turn the bread and cook until the second side is lightly toasted. Rub each side of the toast with a cut side of the garlic.

✪ In a bowl, lightly toss the lettuce with the dressing and place on the bottom of 4 of the toast slices, dividing evenly. Top the lettuce with a patty, Parmesan cheese to taste and the remaining crostini slices. If desired, cut each burger in half. Place the burgers on serving plates and garnish with parsley sprigs.

SERVES 4

15

CARIBBEAN COUSCOUS BURGERS

Sutter Home Winery Build a Better Burger Contest

Third Runner-Up: Richard McHargue · Couscous serves as a binder in Richard's burgers, holding the ingredients together. But it also adds an intriguing texture to his beef and lamb burgers, which are spiked with Caribbean-style spices. The mango salsa is a snap to make and can add zip to any type of grilled poultry, meat or fish.

MANGO SALSA

1 cup diced fresh mango

1/2 cup chopped red bell pepper

1/2 cup diced pineapple

2 tablespoons chopped fresh cilantro

2 tablespoons Sutter Home Zinfandel

1 tablespoon brown sugar

1/4 teaspoon cayenne pepper

BURGERS

1/2 cup Sutter Home Zinfandel

1/3 cup couscous (uncooked)

1 pound ground lamb

1/2 pound ground beef chuck

1/2 cup chopped roasted red bell pepper

1 teaspoon dried thyme

1 teaspoon ground allspice

1/2 teaspoon paprika

1/4 teaspoon cayenne pepper

Vegetable oil

4 slices Kraft Deluxe Old English cheese

4 seeded hamburger buns

Melted butter

Spinach leaves

✪ In a kettle-type grill, prepare a medium-hot charcoal fire.

✪ For the salsa, combine all of the ingredients in a medium bowl and toss lightly. Cover and chill until ready to serve.

✪ For the burgers, place the wine in a small saucepan and bring to a boil directly on the grill rack or on the stovetop. Stir in the couscous, cover and remove from the heat. Let stand for 5 minutes, or until the liquid is absorbed.

✪ In a large bowl, combine the ground lamb, ground chuck, red pepper, thyme, allspice, paprika, cayenne pepper and couscous; mix well with your hands. Divide the mixture into 4 equal portions. Form the portions into patties the same size as the buns.

✪ Brush the grill rack with vegetable oil. Place the patties on the grill. Cover the grill and cook the patties for 5 minutes per side, until the juices run clear when the patties are pierced with the tip of a paring knife. During the last few minutes of cooking, top each patty with a cheese slice.

✪ Brush the buns with melted butter. Place the buns buttered-side down on the grill and cook for about 1 minute, until they are lightly toasted.

✪ Arrange the spinach leaves on the bottom half of the buns. Top the spinach with the cooked patties, a spoonful of salsa and the top half of the buns.

SERVES 4

CASHEW-CRUSTED CATFISH WITH TOMATO-BASIL CREAM

The Catfish Institute's On-Line Consumer Recipe Contest

*Courtesy of The Catfish Institute · To grind the cashews, place them in
a food processor and process in short bursts until a loose, dry texture is achieved. Take care not
to overprocess the nuts—you don't want to end up with nut butter.*

TOMATO-BASIL CREAM

3 tablespoons olive oil

1/2 cup minced onion

4 cloves garlic, minced

2 cups canned crushed tomatoes

1/4 cup homemade chicken stock or
canned chicken broth

1/4 cup heavy cream

1/4 cup minced fresh basil leaves

2 cups cashews, ground

2 teaspoons garlic powder

1 teaspoon cayenne pepper

1/2 teaspoon dried basil

1/2 teaspoon freshly ground black pepper

2 eggs, beaten

1/2 cup milk

2 U.S. farm-raised catfish fillets

Vegetable oil for frying

✪ For the tomato-basil cream, heat the olive oil in a medium saucepan over medium heat. Add the onion and garlic and sauté until transparent.

✪ Add the crushed tomatoes and chicken stock and bring to a boil over high heat.

✪ Reduce the heat to low and simmer for 20 minutes, until the mixture is reduced slightly.

✪ Add the cream and simmer for 5 minutes. Stir in the basil and set aside.

✪ Mix the cashews, garlic powder, cayenne, dried basil and black pepper in a shallow dish or on a piece of waxed paper.

✪ In another shallow dish, beat the eggs with the milk.

✪ Dip the catfish fillets into the egg mixture, letting the excess drip back into the dish. Then, dredge the coated fillets with the cashew mixture, shaking slightly to remove the excess. Set the coated fillets on a waxed paper-lined baking sheet.

✪ Pour 1/2 inch of oil into a large skillet and heat over medium heat. Place the fillets in the hot oil and fry for 5 to 6 minutes on each side, or until the fish flakes easily when tested with a fork.

✪ Place the fillets on each of 2 serving plates and spoon the sauce over the top. Serve immediately.

SERVES 2

CATFISH WRAPS WITH GADO GADO SAUCE

The Catfish Institute's On-Line Consumer Recipe Contest

Courtesy of The Catfish Institute • Look for lemon grass in the produce department of a well-stocked supermarket or in an Asian market. Before using, trim the dry outer skin from the lemon grass stalk; use just the center for the recipe. If desired, you can substitute purchased Thai peanut sauce or teriyaki sauce for the Malaysian-style gado gado sauce.

MARINADE
1 stalk lemon grass, trimmed, or
   1 teaspoon grated fresh lemon zest
1/2 cup canned coconut milk
4 thin slices fresh ginger
1 clove garlic
2 teaspoons lime juice
Grated zest of 1 lime
Salt and cayenne pepper to taste

4 small U.S. farm-raised catfish fillets

GADO GADO SAUCE
1 stalk lemon grass, trimmed, or
   1 teaspoon grated fresh lemon zest
1 tablespoon minced garlic
1 tablespoon lime juice
4 teaspoons soy sauce
2 tablespoons pineapple juice concentrate
2 medium shallots
1/2 cup peanut butter
1/2 cup canned coconut milk
Boiling water, if needed

Four 9- or 10-inch flour tortillas
8 ounces carrots, shredded
8 ounces bean sprouts
1/2 cup fresh mint leaves
1/2 cup fresh basil leaves
1/2 cup fresh watercress

✪ For the marinade, slice the lemon grass finely, if using. Combine the lemon grass or lemon zest, coconut milk, ginger, garlic, lime juice, lime zest, salt and cayenne in a small bowl.

✪ Place the catfish fillets in a shallow dish and add the marinade, turning to coat well. Refrigerate for at least 30 minutes or up to 2 hours.

✪ For the gado gado sauce, smash the lemon grass stalk and place it, or the lemon zest, in a mini-food processor with the garlic, lime juice, soy sauce, pineapple juice concentrate and shallots. Process until finely minced.

✪ Add the peanut butter and coconut milk and process until the mixture is the consistency of thin mayonnaise. Add a few tablespoons of boiling water if the mixture is too thick. The sauce may thicken while standing.

✪ Transfer the catfish fillets and 2 tablespoons of the marinade to a microwave-safe dish. Cover loosely with plastic wrap and microwave at high (100%) power for 5 to 6 minutes, or until just opaque throughout. Let stand until cool. Drain off any liquid and cut the fillets into strips.

✪ Spread one side of each tortilla lightly with gado gado sauce. Place the catfish strips, carrots and sprouts onto the tortilla. Drizzle 2 tablespoons of the sauce over the filling and top with the mint, basil and watercress. Fold in opposite sides of the tortilla one inch over the filling, then roll up securely.

✪ Serve the wraps immediately at room temperature, or refrigerate and serve chilled.

MAKES 4 WRAPS

Catfish Stuffed with Basil-Olive Pesto

The Catfish Institute's On-Line Consumer Recipe Contest

Courtesy of The Catfish Institute · To pit kalamata olives, place them on a cutting board and whack them with the side of a large knife. Squeeze the olives firmly with your fingers to extrude the pits.

BASIL-OLIVE PESTO

2 cloves garlic, coarsely chopped

2 cups fresh basil leaves

1/3 cup pine nuts

1/4 cup olive oil

1/4 cup freshly grated Parmesan cheese

1/4 cup kalamata olives, pitted and chopped

Four 5-ounce U.S. Farm-raised catfish fillets

Salt and freshly ground black pepper to taste

1/2 cup dry white wine

One 4-ounce container mascarpone cheese, or 4 ounces heavy cream

1/2 cup canned roasted red bell peppers, drained and finely chopped

Freshly grated Parmesan cheese for garnish (optional)

Grated lemon zest for garnish (optional)

Fresh basil sprigs for garnish (optional)

Kalamata olives for garnish (optional)

✪ Preheat the oven to 350 degrees.

✪ Make the pesto: In a blender or food processor, combine the garlic, basil leaves, pine nuts and olive oil and process until very finely chopped. Add the Parmesan cheese and chopped olives and pulse briefly until just combined.

✪ Season the catfish fillets with salt and pepper.

✪ Reserve 1/3 of the pesto. Spread the remaining 2/3 of the pesto evenly over the flat side of each fillet. Starting at the tail end, roll the catfish fillets so that the pesto is on the inside; secure the rolls with a toothpick. Arrange the rolls sideways in a shallow ovenproof pan so that they do not touch each other.

✪ Pour the wine around the fillets and cover the dish with foil.

✪ Bake the fillets for 20 to 25 minutes, or until the fish flakes easily. Remove the fish from the pan and keep warm; reserve the liquid in the pan.

✪ Place the pan on the stovetop and bring the cooking liquid to a boil. Cook it until reduced by half, stirring occasionally.

✪ Stir in the mascarpone cheese or cream, the peppers and reserved 1/3 of the pesto; adjust the seasonings.

✪ Divide the sauce among 4 serving plates. Arrange a fish roll in the center of the sauce on each plate. Sprinkle each fillet with garnishes of your choice: Parmesan cheese, lemon zest, basil sprigs and olives.

SERVES 4

Raspberry Walnut Shortbread Bars

Maine State Fair Cookie Contest

1997 National Grand Prize Recipe: Courtesy, Land O'Lakes, Inc. • Here's a quick dessert that uses ingredients that you may already have in your pantry.

CRUST

1 1/4 cups all-purpose flour

1/2 cup sugar

1/2 cup LAND O'LAKES® Butter

TOPPING

1/2 cup raspberry jam

1/3 cup firmly packed brown sugar

2 eggs

1 teaspoon vanilla extract

3 tablespoons all-purpose flour

1/8 teaspoon salt

1 cup chopped walnuts

✪ Preheat the oven to 350 degrees.

✪ In a medium bowl combine 1 1/4 cups flour and the sugar. With a pastry blender cut in the butter until crumbly. Press on the bottom of a greased 9-inch square baking pan.

✪ Bake for 18 to 20 minutes or until the edges are lightly golden brown. Spread the jam over the crust.

✪ In a small mixer bowl combine the brown sugar, eggs and vanilla. Beat at medium speed until well mixed (1 to 2 minutes). Stir in 3 tablespoons flour and the salt until well mixed. Stir in the walnuts.

✪ Pour over the jam; spread carefully to cover. Continue baking for 20 to 24 minutes or until golden brown and the filling is set.

✪ Cool completely and cut into bars.

MAKES 24 BARS

ROESTI | SWISS FRIED POTATOES

Green County Cheese Days

*Reprinted from "Old World Swiss Family Recipes": Pat Waterman and
Gloria Jacobson · The amounts of potatoes, onions and cheese can be altered to suit your taste.
For best results, boil the potatoes the day before you shred them.*

1/4 cup butter

1 onion, chopped (optional)

6 to 8 russet potatoes, boiled, peeled and shredded

1/2 cup shredded Swiss, Gruyère or Emmentaller cheese, plus more if desired

Salt and freshly ground black pepper to taste

✪ In a skillet, melt the butter over medium heat. Add the onion and sauté until translucent.

✪ Add the potatoes and cheese and stir until well mixed. Cook without stirring for 5 to 10 minutes, until a golden crust has formed on the bottom.

✪ Turn the pancake with a large spatula, pressing down slightly. Cook on the other side and season with salt and pepper.

✪ Add additional cheese, if necessary, and cook until melted. Serve immediately.

SERVES 8 TO 12

KAESEKUCHEN | CHEESE AND ONION PIE

Green County Cheese Days

Reprinted from "Old World Swiss Family Recipes": Trudi Thomann · similar to a quiche, this dish can be served any time of the day. If featuring it at lunch or dinner, accompany it by a tossed green salad.

One 9-inch pie shell (unbaked)

$1/4$ pound bacon, cooked and crumbled

1 large onion, chopped and sautéed until translucent

$3/4$ cup grated Swiss cheese

$3/4$ cup grated Gruyère cheese

3 eggs, well beaten

$1/2$ cup milk

$1/2$ cup cream or half-and-half

Salt and ground nutmeg to taste

Paprika

✪ Line a 9-inch pie pan with the pie shell.

✪ Place $1/3$ each of the bacon and onion in the pastry and top with half of the cheeses.

✪ Top the cheese with another $1/3$ each of the bacon and onion and top with the remaining half of the cheeses.

✪ Top the cheese with the remaining $1/3$ of the bacon and onion.

✪ In a bowl, mix the eggs with the milk, cream, salt and nutmeg and pour over the bacon, onion and cheese.

✪ Place the mixture in the refrigerator for 30 minutes. While the mixture is chilling, preheat the oven to 400 degrees.

✪ Remove the pie from the oven, sprinkle with paprika and bake for 30 minutes. Turn off the oven and let the pie stand in the oven for 15 more minutes.

✪ Remove the pie from the oven. Cut into wedges to serve.

SERVES 6 TO 8

SWISS CHEESE FONDUE

Green County Cheese Days

Reprinted from "Old World Swiss Family Recipes": Deborah Krauss Smith · Use any type of Swiss cheese for this homey dish, such as Gruyère or Emmentaller.

1 pound Swiss cheese, coarsely grated

2 tablespoons cornstarch

1/2 teaspoon salt

1/4 teaspoon ground white pepper

1/4 teaspoon ground nutmeg

2 cups buttermilk

1 clove garlic

1 loaf French bread, cut into cubes

✪ In a large bowl, toss the cheese with the cornstarch, salt, pepper and nutmeg.

✪ In a fondue pot, heat the buttermilk with the garlic over low heat. When hot, remove and discard the garlic.

✪ Add the cheese mixture to the fondue pot and heat, stirring frequently, until the cheese is melted.

✪ To serve, place the bread cubes in a serving bowl. Let guests dip the bread cubes into the hot cheese mixture using long-handled fondue forks.

SERVES 4 TO 6

CHEESE DAYS DEEP-FRIED CHEESE CURDS

Green County Cheese Days

*Reprinted from "Wisconsin Food Festivals": Terese Allen · During cheesemaking,
milk separates into solid portions (curds) and liquid portions (whey). Though cheese curds aren't
really used for this recipe, you can achieve nearly the same results by using a very young cheddar
cheese, which can be obtained from a good-quality cheese purveyor.*

Vegetable oil

1 1/2 cups purchased pancake mix

1/2 cup stale beer

1 egg, lightly beaten

Scant 1/2 cup water

1 1/2 to 2 pounds young cheddar cheese,
cut into 1-inch cubes

✪ In a large rimmed skillet, heat about 1 1/2 inches of oil until it is about 360 degrees.

✪ Place the pancake mix in a medium bowl.

✪ In another bowl, mix the beer, egg and water until blended and stir into the pancake mix.

✪ Add the cheese cubes to the batter and stir until well coated.

✪ Remove the coated cheese cubes from the batter and place in the hot oil in batches. Fry the cheese cubes until golden brown and puffed; drain on paper towels.

✪ Cool the fried cheese for a few minutes before serving, so that it won't burn tongues.

SERVES 8 TO 12

GOLD MINER'S CHILI

International Chili Society World's Championship Chili Cook-Off and Salsa Contest

1997 Winner: Stephen Falkowski, Hopewell Junction, New York • Stephen's chili has a balance of flavor components—sweet, salty, sour and spicy. The recipe is easy to put together, but it needs a long simmering time to blend the flavors.

1½ cups finely minced white onions

8 cloves garlic, finely minced

Two 15½-ounce cans chicken broth, defatted

4 ounces Hunt's tomato sauce

3 tablespoons ground cumin

10½ tablespoons Gebhardt chili powder
  or 5 tablespoons mild California chili powder
  or 4½ tablespoons medium-hot New Mexico chili powder
  or 1 tablespoon hot New Mexico chili powder

¾ teaspoon garlic powder

2 teaspoons salt

3 pounds beef, cut into ¼-inch cubes

1 tablespoon vegetable oil

½ teaspoon light brown sugar

1 teaspoon Tabasco sauce

✪ In a large, heavy-bottomed pot, simmer the onions and minced garlic in 2 cups of the chicken broth for 10 minutes. Add the tomato sauce, cumin, chili powder, garlic powder and salt and mix well.

✪ In a skillet, cook the beef cubes in the vegetable oil until browned on all sides. Drain the meat well and add to the pot. Add the remaining chicken broth to the pot and simmer the mixture for 2½ hours.

✪ Add the brown sugar and Tabasco just before serving.

SERVES 6 TO 10

24-Karat Chili

International Chili Society World's Championship Chili Cook-Off and Salsa Contest

1998 Winner: Kathy LeGear, Dallas, Texas · Layers of spices are the secret to the winning flavor of Kathy's traditional-style beef chili.

2 teaspoons vegetable oil

2½ pounds beef roast, cubed

Two 10-ounce cans beef broth

2 cups water

Two 8-ounce cans Hunt's tomato sauce

FIRST SPICES

1 teaspoon MSG (optional)

2 tablespoons onion powder

2 teaspoons beef bouillon granules

1 teaspoon chicken bouillon granules

1 teaspoon garlic powder

¼ teaspoon seasoned salt

1 tablespoon paprika

1 tablespoon Texas chili powder

1 tablespoon ground chili pepper

SECOND SPICES

1 teaspoon MSG (optional)

2 teaspoons ground cumin

1 teaspoon garlic powder

¼ teaspoon seasoned salt

1 tablespoon Texas chili powder

1 tablespoon Gebhardt chili powder

THIRD SPICES

1½ teaspoons ground cumin

½ teaspoon garlic powder

1 tablespoon Texas chili powder

1 tablespoon Gebhardt chili powder

FOURTH SPICES

1½ teaspoons ground cumin

1 tablespoon Texas chili powder

½ teaspoon garlic powder

Salt to taste

Tabasco sauce to taste

✪ In a large heavy-bottomed pot, heat the vegetable oil over medium-high heat. Add the beef and cook until browned on all sides. Add the beef broth, water, 1 can of the tomato sauce and the first spices. Bring the mixture to a boil over high heat. Cover, reduce heat slightly and simmer for about 2 hours.

✪ Add the remaining can of tomato sauce and the second spices to the pot and simmer for 10 minutes.

✪ Add the third spices and simmer for 10 minutes.

✪ Add the fourth spices and simmer for 10 minutes.

✪ Taste and add salt and Tabasco sauce. The chili is done when the beef is cooked through and very tender.

SERVES 4 TO 6

B&M's Double Flush Salsa

International Chili Society World's Championship Chili Cook-Off and Salsa Contest

1998 Winner: Bonnie Ford, La Mirada, California · Jalapeños can vary in heat from crop to crop. You can add them to Bonnie's version of tomato salsa a little at a time if you're concerned about the heat.

3 pounds Roma tomatoes, seeded and coarsely chopped

1/4 pound jalapeño peppers, seeded and finely chopped

3/4 pound Maui onions or other sweet onions, finely chopped

Leaves from 3 bunches fresh cilantro, finely chopped

2 teaspoons granulated garlic

1/8 teaspoon green chili powder

1/8 teaspoon Tabasco sauce, plus more to taste

2 tablespoons vegetable oil

3 tablespoons red wine vinegar

2 tablespoons lime juice

1/2 teaspoon freshly ground black pepper

1 tablespoon garlic salt

1 medium avocado

Salt to taste

✪ In a bowl, combine the tomatoes, peppers, onions, cilantro, granulated garlic, chili powder, Tabasco, oil, vinegar, lime juice, pepper and garlic salt. Mix gently until combined.

✪ Just before serving, peel and pit the avocado and cut into medium dice. Add to the salsa mixture and mix gently.

✪ Add Tabasco and salt to taste.

MAKES ABOUT 4 CUPS

STONEY ROAD TOMATO SALSA

International Chili Society World's Championship Chili Cook-Off and Salsa Contest

*1997 Winner: Le Ann Nienow, Sacramento, California • Anaheims,
a mild variety of peppers, make Le Ann's salsa a tame one. You should be able to find
Anaheims in any supermarket's produce section.*

3 long, green Anaheim peppers, seeded,
  ribs removed and diced

2 yellow bell peppers, seeded,
  ribs removed and diced

8 fresh tomatoes, seeded and diced

1 medium-sized red onion, diced

2 green onions, sliced

1 clove garlic, minced

1 tablespoon rice vinegar

1 tablespoon fresh lime juice

1 teaspoon sugar

1 teaspoon olive oil

1/4 to 1/2 cup minced fresh cilantro leaves

Salt to taste

Tomato juice (optional)

Diced avocado (optional)

Diced cucumber (optional)

✪ In a bowl, combine the peppers, tomatoes, onions and garlic and mix well.

✪ Add the vinegar, lime juice, sugar, olive oil, cilantro and salt and mix gently until blended.

✪ If the mixture is too thick for your taste, thin with a little tomato juice.

✪ Stir in diced avocado or cucumber to taste, if desired.

MAKES ABOUT 6 CUPS

CORN LIGHT BREAD

Reprinted from "Jack Daniel's The Spirit of Tennessee Cookbook" (Rutledge Hill Press): Lynne Tolley and Pat Mitchamore · Use a loaf pan with a dark, dull finish if you prefer a crisper crust for your cornbread. This cornbread is an apt companion to chili or barbecued meats.

2 cups cornmeal

1 cup all-purpose flour

$\frac{1}{2}$ cup sugar

1 teaspoon baking soda

1 teaspoon salt

3 tablespoons bacon drippings

2 cups buttermilk

✪ Preheat the oven to 300 degrees. Grease and flour a 9-x-5-x-3-inch loaf pan.

✪ In a bowl, stir together the cornmeal, flour, sugar, soda and salt. Add the bacon drippings and buttermilk and beat well.

✪ Pour the batter into the prepared pan. Bake the bread for 1 hour and 15 minutes, until the bread is golden brown.

✪ Remove the pan from the oven and cool.

MAKES 1 LOAF

CRANBERRY BALSAMIC CHICKEN WITH PORTOBELLOS, RICE PILAF AND SPICED SWEET POTATOES

Massachusetts Cranberry Harvest Festival

First Prize/Best of Show: Bernadette Cicione, Courtesy of the Massachusetts Cranberry Harvest Festival · Bernadette's chicken mixture is also tasty served over cooked pasta, mashed white potatoes or toast points.

3 large portobello mushroom caps

1/2 cup jellied cranberry sauce

1 cup water

5 tablespoons olive oil

2 1/2 pounds boneless chicken breast tenders, cut into 2-inch chunks

6 green onions, white and green parts, chopped

1 1/2 cups fresh or frozen whole cranberries

1/4 cup balsamic vinegar

1/4 cup soy sauce

1 1/2 cups packed dark brown sugar

3 tablespoons cornstarch

1 cup sweetened dried cranberries

RICE PILAF

1 cup long-grain rice (uncooked)

1/2 cup chopped pecans, toasted

1/2 cup sweetened dried cranberries

✪ With a damp paper towel, wipe off any visible dirt from the top of the mushroom caps. Cut each cap into quarters and slice the quarters into 1/2-inch-thick pieces. Set aside.

✪ In a bowl, whisk the cranberry sauce with the water until smooth. Set aside.

✪ In a large skillet, heat the olive oil over medium heat for about 30 seconds. Add the chicken pieces and cook, covered, until cooked through, stirring occasionally.

✪ Reduce the heat to low. With a slotted spoon, transfer the chicken to a plate, leaving the juices in the pan.

✪ Increase the heat to medium-low and add the green onions, mushroom pieces and whole cranberries. Sauté the mixture for 2 to 3 minutes, until the cranberries are soft.

✪ Add the vinegar, soy sauce, cranberry-water mixture and brown sugar. Stir to dissolve the sugar completely. Add the cornstarch and whisk until completely dissolved. Simmer the sauce, stirring constantly, for about 30 seconds, until thickened. Reduce the heat to low and continue stirring.

✪ Return the chicken to the pan and stir until completely coated with the sauce. Cover the pan and simmer for 2 to 3 minutes, until heated through.

SPICED SWEET POTATOES

2 large sweet potatoes, baked

3 tablespoons butter

1/3 cup packed dark brown sugar

1/2 teaspoon ground cinnamon

Pinch ground nutmeg

1/8 teaspoon cayenne pepper

1/4 cup evaporated milk

Pinch freshly ground black pepper

1/4 cup sweetened dried cranberries

✪ Remove the chicken mixture from the heat, add the dried cranberries and mix well. Keep warm.

✪ For the rice pilaf, cook the rice according to package directions. Stir in the toasted pecans and dried cranberries.

✪ For the spiced sweet potatoes, cool the baked sweet potatoes until cool enough to handle. With a paring knife, remove the peels from the potatoes. Discard the peels. Place the sweet potato flesh in a bowl and mash until smooth.

✪ Add the butter and mix well. Add the brown sugar, cinnamon, nutmeg and cayenne and mix well.

✪ Add the evaporated milk and whisk until well mixed. Season with pepper. Add the dried cranberries and mix well.

✪ To serve, place a mound of sweet potatoes in the center of each serving plate. With the back of a spoon, make a well in the center of the mound and build up the sides.

✪ Place a portion of the rice in the well. Spoon the chicken-mushroom mixture over the rice.

SERVES 4 TO 6

NOTE: This dish can be made a day in advance and heated through when ready to serve.

CRANBERRY PINEAPPLE TORTE

Massachusetts Cranberry Harvest Festival

First Prize: Lorraine Carr, New Bedford, Massachusetts, Courtesy of the Massachusetts Cranberry Harvest Festival • Lorraine's cake takes a little prep time, but the results will dazzle your guests.

CAKE

2 cups all-purpose flour

1 tablespoon baking powder

1/2 teaspoon salt

1 1/2 cups sugar

1/2 cup vegetable oil

1/2 cup water

7 eggs, separated, at room temperature

1/2 teaspoon cream of tartar

FILLING

One 20-ounce can crushed pineapple in syrup

3 cups fresh or frozen cranberries

1 cup sugar

1 cup chopped walnuts

✪ Preheat the oven to 325 degrees. Grease three 8-inch round cake pans and line the bottoms of the pans with greased waxed paper.

✪ For the cake, sift together the flour, baking powder, salt and sugar into a large bowl. Gradually add the oil, water and egg yolks, beating until well mixed.

✪ In another bowl, beat the egg whites with the cream of tartar until stiff peaks form, but the mixture is not dry.

✪ Add a small amount of egg whites to the batter and gently fold together until mixed. Then, add the batter to the egg whites and fold together until well mixed.

✪ Spoon about 1 cup of the batter into each prepared cake pan, spreading evenly. Bake the cake layers for about 8 to 10 minutes, or until the cake begins to pull away from the sides of the pans.

✪ Remove the cake layers from the oven and invert onto wire racks. Remove the waxed paper and cool completely.

✪ When cake pans are completely cool, prepare them as directed above and continue baking with the remaining batter; you should have 6 layers total.

✪ For the filling, combine all the ingredients in a saucepan and cook over medium heat until the berries pop and the mixture starts to thicken. Drain through a sieve. (Discard the liquid, or save it as a flavoring for ginger ale or iced tea, or as a sauce for cake, ice cream or pudding.) Cool the cranberry mixture completely.

FROSTING

½ cup butter, at room temperature

½ cup vegetable shortening

1 cup superfine sugar

1 cup milk

¼ cup all-purpose flour

1 teaspoon vanilla extract

✪ For the frosting, beat the butter and shortening with a mixer until fluffy. Gradually add the sugar, beating for about 5 minutes.

✪ In a saucepan, combine the milk and flour. Cook, stirring constantly, over medium heat until thickened. Remove the mixture from the heat and cool to room temperature.

✪ Gradually add the milk mixture to the sugar mixture and beat until light and fluffy and no sugar granules remain. Add the vanilla and beat until well mixed.

✪ To assemble, place one cake layer on a serving plate. Spread with one-third of the cranberry filling. Top with another cake layer and spread with one-forth of the frosting. Repeat the layering process until all of the cake layers and cranberry filling are used, ending with a layer of frosting.

✪ Frost the sides of the cake with the remaining one-fourth of the frosting.

✪ Cut the cake into wedges to serve.

SERVES 10 TO 12

DUTCH-STYLE PEA SOUP

Historic Menu from the Greenfield Village and Henry Ford Museum

Courtesy of the Greenfield Village and Henry Ford Museum · This recipe makes a lot of soup, perfect for feeding a crowd. If you a serving just a few, cut the ingredients in half or freeze the extras. Serve the soup with hunks of crusty bread.

3 cups dried green peas

2 to 3 cups water

4 quarts water, plus more if needed

1½ tablespoons salt

1½ pounds shredded cooked pork

6 small potatoes

3 large onions, sliced

Water to thin soup, if needed

✪ In a large, heavy bottomed saucepan, bring the peas and 2 to 3 cups water to a boil; boil for 10 minutes.

✪ While the peas are boiling, bring the 4 quarts water to a boil in a stockpot.

✪ Drain the peas and add them to the stockpot with the boiling water. Simmer over medium heat for 30 minutes.

✪ Add the salt and shredded pork and continue cooking for 30 more minutes.

✪ Peel the potatoes and cut into small cubes. Add the onions and potato cubes to the stockpot and cook over low heat for 30 more minutes. If the soup seems too thick, add more water.

SERVES 16

SAUERKRAUT DRESSING FOR ROASTED POULTRY

Historic Menu from the Greenfield Village and Henry Ford Museum

Courtesy of the Greenfield Village and Henry Ford Museum • Follow your favorite recipe for roasted turkey, goose or duck, but replace the stuffing with this tangy version. It will fill a 10- to 12-pound turkey or goose. Or, cut the recipe in half to stuff a 5-pound duck.

1/2 cup butter

1/4 cup flour

5 cups prepared sauerkraut

2 large tart apples, finely chopped

1/2 cup cider vinegar

6 whole cloves

1/4 cup brown sugar

✪ In a skillet, melt the butter over medium-low heat. Add the flour and stir until smooth. Add the sauerkraut, apples, vinegar, cloves and brown sugar. Mix well and cool completely before stuffing the poultry.

MAKES ABOUT 6 CUPS

POTATO PUDDING

Historic Menu from the Greenfield Village and Henry Ford Museum

Courtesy of the Greenfield Village and Henry Ford Museum · In the 1700s, this side dish would have replaced today's mashed potatoes. It is a sweet dish, a bit like candied yams, and can even be served as an unusual dessert. When separating the eggs, plan ahead: You will use all seven of the egg yolks, but only four of the egg whites.

1 pound russet potatoes, peeled, boiled and mashed

½ cup butter or margarine

¾ to 1 cup milk, cream or half-and-half

1½ cups sugar

7 eggs, separated (reserve 3 egg whites for another use)

1½ teaspoons vanilla extract

½ teaspoon ground nutmeg (optional)

✪ Preheat the oven to 350 degrees. Grease a 2- to 3-quart baking dish.

✪ In a bowl, combine the mashed potatoes and butter or margarine and mix until smooth.

✪ Slowly add the milk, then the sugar, stirring until well mixed.

✪ Add the 7 egg yolks, 4 egg whites, vanilla and nutmeg, if using, and stir until well mixed. Pour the mixture into the dish.

✪ Bake the pudding for 30 to 45 minutes, or until a knife inserted into the center comes out clean. Serve warm.

SERVES 8

GINGERBREAD CAKE

Historic Menu from the Greenfield Village and Henry Ford Museum

Courtesy of the Greenfield Village and Henry Ford Museum · The batter for this spice-infused cake is very thick. Serve the cake slightly warm for breakfast or dessert.

3/4 cup plus 1 tablespoon margarine

Heaping 1 1/4 cups sugar

2 eggs

1 egg yolk

5 1/4 cups cake flour

1/2 teaspoon salt

1 1/4 teaspoons baking soda

1 1/4 teaspoons ground cinnamon

1 3/4 teaspoons ground ginger

1 1/4 teaspoons ground allspice

1 1/4 cups light molasses

1 1/4 cups buttermilk

✪ Preheat the oven to 350 degrees. Grease and lightly flour a 10-inch round cake pan.

✪ In a large bowl, beat the margarine and sugar until light and fluffy. Add the eggs and egg yolk and mix well.

✪ In a small bowl, mix together the flour, salt, baking soda, cinnamon, ginger and allspice.

✪ In another small bowl, mix the molasses with the buttermilk.

✪ Add the flour mixture to the egg mixture alternately with the buttermilk mixture and mix well.

✪ Pour the batter into the prepared pan and bake for 25 to 30 minutes, until a toothpick inserted into the center comes out clean.

SERVES 20

GARLIC SPRING ROLLS WITH GARLICKY LIME SAUCE

Gilroy Garlic Festival

1998 Finalist: Kim Landhuis, Fort Dodge, Iowa • Look for spring roll wrappers and fish sauce, which Kim calls for in her recipe, in an Asian food market.

DIPPING SAUCE

20 cloves garlic

2/3 cup fresh lime juice

1/4 cup Vietnamese fish sauce (nuoc mam)

1/4 cup diced jalapeño peppers

2 teaspoons sugar

FILLING

15 cloves garlic

1/2 cup chopped water chestnuts

2 cups ground pork

5 green onions, chopped

1/2 cup grated carrot

2 teaspoons sugar

1 teaspoon salt

1 teaspoon coarsely ground black pepper

4 cups thinly sliced napa cabbage

18 spring roll wrappers, thawed if frozen

Canola oil

Boston lettuce leaves for garnish (optional)

Pickled carrots for garnish (optional)

Green onion brushes for garnish (optional)

✪ To make the dipping sauce, place the garlic in a food processor and process until finely chopped. Transfer to a bowl with the remaining ingredients and mix well; set aside.

✪ For the filling, place the garlic in a food processor and process until finely chopped. Transfer the garlic to a large bowl.

✪ Add the water chestnuts, pork, chopped green onions, grated carrot, sugar, salt and pepper and mix well. Add the cabbage and fold gently into the mixture.

✪ To assemble the spring rolls, lightly dust a work surface with cornstarch. Place 1 of the spring roll wrappers on the work surface and rub the edges with a wet finger. Place about 2 tablespoons of the filling into the center of the wrapper.

✪ Fold one corner of the wrapper up over the filling. Fold in the sides of the wrapper and roll up tightly to the remaining corner to seal in the filling.

✪ Repeat the filling and rolling procedures with the rest of the pork filling and wrappers.

✪ In a large rimmed skillet or wok, heat about 1/4 inch of oil over medium-high heat. Add the spring rolls in batches and fry until golden brown on all sides; drain on paper towels and keep warm.

✪ To serve, arrange the spring rolls on a platter with a bowl of dipping sauce in the middle. Garnish with lettuce leaves, pickled carrot and green onion brushes, if desired.

SERVES 6

FLAMBOYANT FLANK STEAK WITH FRAGRANT FILLING

Gilroy Garlic Festival

1998 Finalist: Frances Benthin, Scio, Oregon · Roasting garlic transforms its assertive flavor into a mellow, nutty paste. Combined with creamy mascarpone cheese (available at specialty food stores) and seasonings, it makes a nifty filling for Frances' grilled marinated steak pinwheels.

MARINADE

6 cloves garlic

¼ cup hoisin sauce

¼ cup dry red wine

2 tablespoons honey

2 tablespoons toasted sesame oil

1 tablespoon chopped fresh rosemary

One flank steak, about 1½ pounds

FILLING

2 bulbs garlic, roasted (see NOTE)

½ cup dry bread crumbs

¼ cup finely chopped roasted red bell pepper

¼ cup mascarpone cheese

2 tablespoons Dijon-style mustard

½ teaspoon seasoned salt

¼ teaspoon cayenne pepper

Chopped fresh garlic for garnish

Rosemary sprigs for garnish

Roasted red bell pepper strips for garnish

✪ For the marinade, combine all ingredients in a blender and process until smooth.

✪ With a knife, score the flank steak in a diamond pattern on both sides. Place the steak in a heavy-duty locking plastic bag with the marinade and seal the bag well. Refrigerate the steak for at least 1 hour, turning the bag occasionally.

✪ For the filling, squeeze the roasted garlic from the skins into a bowl. Add the remaining filling ingredients and mix well.

✪ Prepare a medium-hot barbecue fire or heat the broiler.

✪ When ready to cook, remove the steak from the marinade and pat dry with paper towels. Place the steak flat on a work surface. Spread the filling evenly over the steak.

✪ Starting from the long edge of the steak, roll the steak tightly, jelly roll-fashion. With a knife, cut the steak into 6 equal pieces and secure each piece with a skewer.

✪ Grill or broil the steak pieces for about 3 to 4 minutes per side, or until the steak is the desired doneness.

✪ Garnish servings with chopped garlic, rosemary sprigs and red pepper strips.

SERVES 6

NOTE: To roast garlic, cut off about ¼ inch from the top of the garlic bulbs. Place the garlic bulbs on a sheet of aluminum foil and drizzle with olive oil. Sprinkle lightly with salt and freshly ground black pepper and wrap with the foil. Bake in a 350 degree oven for about 30 minutes, until the garlic pulp is soft.

BAKED STUFFED PORTOBELLO MUSHROOM CAPS

Gilroy Garlic Festival

1998 Finalist: Margaret Ann Bavaro, Colt's Neck, New Jersey • Portobello mushrooms, though they seem exotic, are actually ordinary brown (or cremini) mushrooms that have been allowed to mature. The extra growing time gives them a deeper flavor than regular-sized mushrooms.

DRESSING

1/4 cup balsamic vinegar

1 clove garlic, finely chopped

1 teaspoon garlic powder

1 teaspoon dried oregano

1/2 teaspoon salt

1/4 teaspoon freshly ground black pepper

1/2 cup olive oil

6 tablespoons olive oil

6 cloves garlic, finely chopped

1/3 cup shredded fresh basil

6 medium portobello mushroom caps
(6 to 8 ounces each)

3/4 cup marinated sun-dried tomatoes

6 oil-cured black olives, pitted

1 teaspoon capers

1 bulb garlic, roasted (see note, page 48),
pulp squeezed from skins

1/3 cup ricotta cheese

1/2 pound mixed baby salad greens

✪ Preheat the oven to 400 degrees.

✪ For the dressing, combine the vinegar, garlic, garlic powder, oregano, salt and pepper. Whisk until blended. Slowly add the oil while whisking until the ingredients are well mixed; set aside.

✪ In a skillet, heat 3 tablespoons of the olive oil over medium-low heat. Add the chopped garlic and 3 tablespoons of the basil and sauté for about 3 minutes, until the garlic is aromatic; remove from heat and set aside.

✪ Place the mushroom caps gill-side down on a greased 11-x-17-inch baking sheet. With a small knife, cut the mushroom caps in half horizontally and reserve the top halves.

✪ In a food processor, combine the tomatoes with the remaining 3 tablespoons olive oil and process until smooth. Add the remaining basil, the olives and capers and process until smooth. Transfer the mixture to a small bowl.

✪ Spread 1/6 of the tomato mixture on the bottom half of each mushroom cap.

✪ In a small bowl, mix the roasted garlic pulp with the ricotta cheese. Spread the ricotta mixture over the tomato mixture, dividing evenly. Top with the reserved mushroom tops.

✪ Drizzle the garlic-basil-oil mixture evenly over the mushrooms. Bake the stuffed mushrooms for about 8 minutes, until tender and hot.

✪ Divide the baby salad greens among 6 serving plates. Top each portion with a baked stuffed mushroom. Whisk the dressing to combine the ingredients and drizzle about 2 tablespoons of the dressing onto each portion. Serve immediately.

SERVES 6

SMOKED SALMON FRITTATA

Eastport Salmon Festival

Jett Peterson, Owner, Weston House Bed and Breakfast, Eastport, Maine · A frittata is an Italian version of an omelet that is baked in the oven rather than cooked on the stovetop. Just as with an omelet, you can use almost anything as a filling. When shopping for smoked salmon, look for the hot-smoked type, which Jett prefers for his frittata.

6 large eggs

1 cup sour cream, plus more for garnish

½ teaspoon salt

½ teaspoon Tabasco sauce, or to taste

¼ cup all-purpose flour

¼ pound smoked salmon, torn into bits

1 cup shredded Gruyère cheese

5 green onions, chopped

2 tablespoons chopped fresh dill, or
   2 teaspoons dried

1 tablespoon butter

Salmon caviar for garnish (optional)

Dill sprigs for garnish

✪ Preheat the oven to 375 degrees.

✪ In a bowl, whisk the eggs with the sour cream, salt and Tabasco. Add the flour and mix until blended. Stir in the smoked salmon, cheese, green onions and dill.

✪ In a 10-inch ovenproof skillet, melt the butter over medium heat until it sizzles. Add the egg mixture. Place the skillet in the oven and bake for 20 minutes, or until the eggs are set and the top is browned.

✪ Cut the frittata into wedges and place on serving plates. Garnish with sour cream, salmon caviar, if using, and a sprig of dill.

SERVES 6 TO 8

SIMPLE GRILLED SALMON

Eastport Salmon Festival

*Courtesy of The Heritage Salmon Company, Eastport, Maine ·
Buying the best-quality salmon steaks you can find ensures success with this dish.
Since it has so few ingredients, the pure flavors shine through.*

1 tablespoon reduced-calorie mayonnaise

1 tablespoon Dijon-style mustard

1 pound fresh Heritage salmon fillets or
   steaks

✪ Preheat the grill or broiler.

✪ In a small bowl, mix the mayonnaise and the mustard. Brush the salmon fillets with the mayonnaise-mustard mixture.

✪ Place the fillets skin-side down on the grill (or skin-side up under the broiler). Cook for 10 to 12 minutes, until the fish flakes easily when tested with a fork.

SERVES 2

GRILLED SALMON WITH MUSTARD AND DILL

Eastport Salmon Festival

*Courtesy of The Heritage Salmon Company, Eastport, Maine · Tangy mustard and
fresh dill are lovely counterpoints to the distinctive flavor of salmon.*

1 pound fresh Heritage salmon fillets or
   steaks

1 tablespoon Dijon-style mustard

1 tablespoon chopped fresh dill, or
   1 teaspoon dried

Freshly ground black pepper to taste

2 tablespoons fresh lime juice

✪ Preheat the grill or broiler.

✪ Place the salmon fillets skin-side down in a shallow dish.

✪ Spread the fillets with the mustard. Sprinkle the fillets with the chopped dill, pepper and lime juice.

✪ Grill (or broil) the salmon for 10 to 12 minutes, until the fish flakes easily when tested with a fork.

SERVES 2

MAPLE-GLAZED ATLANTIC SALMON FILLETS WITH APPLES, GRILLED POTATOES AND BABY CARROTS

Eastport Salmon Festival

Courtesy of the Maine Department of Aqua Resources · For best results, use pure maple syrup, which can be found in better supermarkets and specialty food stores.

3 tablespoons butter

1 tablespoon minced shallots

$1/2$ cup dry white wine

2 tablespoons fresh lemon juice

$1/4$ cup pure maple syrup

3 Cortland apples, cored and cut into wedges

3 to 4 scallions, sliced

1 tablespoon chopped fresh parsley

1 teaspoon grated lemon zest

GRILLED POTATOES

2 potatoes, boiled until just under done

Vegetable oil

Salt and freshly ground black pepper to taste

BABY CARROTS

2 cups whole baby carrots, peeled and trimmed (leave some of the green tops for color)

2 tablespoons butter

2 tablespoons brown sugar

1 teaspoon finely chopped fresh tarragon

Four 6- to 8-ounce Atlantic Salmon fillets or steaks

✪ Preheat the grill or broiler.

✪ In a skillet, melt the butter over medium heat. Add the shallots and sauté for 30 to 40 seconds. Add the wine and reduce by half. Add the lemon juice and maple syrup and simmer for 1 minute. Add the apple wedges, scallions, parsley and lemon zest and sauté for about 2 minutes. Keep warm.

✪ For the potatoes, cut each potato into 6 wedges and brush with oil. Season with salt and pepper. Place the potato wedges on a lightly oiled grill or stovetop grill pan and cook over medium heat until browned and cooked through. Keep warm.

✪ For the carrots, place them in a saucepan and cover with cold water. Bring the water to a boil over high heat. Reduce the heat to low and simmer the carrots for 2 minutes; drain. In a skillet, melt the butter with the brown sugar over medium-low heat. Add the carrots and sauté for about 5 minutes, until they are glazed. Stir in the tarragon.

✪ Grill (or broil) the salmon for 10 to 12 minutes, until the fish flakes easily when tested with a fork.

✪ Arrange the salmon fillets on warmed dinner plates. Divide the apple wedges equally among the plates and top each portion with some of the maple sauce. Divide the potatoes and carrots among the plates and serve immediately.

SERVES 4

GRILLED CITRUS SALMON

Eastport Salmon Festival

Courtesy of The Heritage Salmon Company, Eastport, Maine • Fresh lemon and orange juice lend a clean, bright flavor to simply grilled salmon fillets.

1 pound fresh Heritage salmon fillets or steaks

1 orange

1 lemon

2 teaspoons chopped fresh thyme leaves, or $1/2$ teaspoon dried

Freshly ground black pepper to taste

✪ Preheat the grill or broiler.

✪ Place the salmon skin-side down in a shallow dish.

✪ Cut the orange and lemon in half. Grate the zest from one of the orange halves and one of the lemon halves and place in a small bowl; squeeze the juice of the zested orange half and lemon half into the bowl with the zest; reserve the remaining orange and lemon halves. Mix the juice and the zest and pour over the salmon.

✪ Sprinkle the salmon with thyme and pepper.

✪ Grill (or broil) the salmon for 10 to 12 minutes, until the fish flakes easily when tested with a fork.

✪ Slice the reserved orange half and lemon half and use to garnish the salmon.

SERVES 2

GRILLED SALMON IN TEQUILA-LIME MARINADE WITH TROPICAL FRUIT SALSA AND CARIBBEAN WILD RICE

Eastport Salmon Festival

Courtesy of the Maine Department of Marine Resources • Here salmon and wild rice are perked up with the Latin and Caribbean flavors of tequila, lime and tropical fruits.

3 ounces tequila

2 tablespoons fresh lime juice

2 teaspoons grated lime zest

2 tablespoons chopped fresh cilantro

3 tablespoons olive oil

Four 6- to 8-ounce Atlantic salmon fillets
   or steaks

1/2 teaspoon salt

1 tablespoon freshly ground black pepper

TROPICAL FRUIT SALSA

1 large banana, diced

1 1/2 teaspoons fresh lime juice

1/2 cup diced peeled fresh peach

1/2 cup diced peeled fresh mango

1/2 cup diced peeled fresh pineapple

1 tablespoon finely diced red onion

1/2 cup diced red bell pepper

2 tablespoons chopped fresh cilantro

2 tablespoons minced peeled fresh ginger

1 1/2 teaspoons olive oil

2 tablespoons prepared banana chutney
   (Busha Brownes preferred)

1 teaspoon hot pepper sauce, or 2
   tablespoons diced jalapeño, or use
   both

CARIBBEAN WILD RICE

4 cups water

6 ounces wild rice

1 tablespoon chopped onion

1/2 cup dried mixed tropical fruits

2 tablespoons each almonds and pecans, toasted

1 tablespoon chopped fresh chives

✪ In a shallow baking dish, combine the tequila, lime juice, lime zest, cilantro and olive oil. Add the salmon fillets and turn to coat with the marinade. Cover the dish with plastic wrap and refrigerate for 2 hours.

✪ Preheat the grill or broiler.

✪ Remove the salmon from the marinade and season with salt and pepper. Grill or broil the salmon for about 5 to 6 minutes on each side, until the fish flakes easily when tested with a fork.

✪ For the salsa, combine the diced banana with the lime juice in a bowl. Add the peach, mango and pineapple and mix well. Add the onion, pepper, cilantro, ginger, olive oil, chutney, and hot sauce and mix well. Cover and chill until ready to use.

✪ For the rice, bring the water to a boil in a medium saucepan. Stir in the rice and the onion and reduce the heat to low. Simmer covered for 45 to 60 minutes, until most of the kernels have burst open. If necessary, drain the excess water from the rice. Fluff the grains with a fork. Add the dried fruit, nuts and chives and stir until well mixed. Let stand for about 5 minutes.

✪ To serve, divide the rice among 4 heated dinner plates. Arrange a salmon portion on each plate and top with the salsa.

SERVES 4

FAT BOYS' BARBECUE BRISKET

Jack Daniel's World Championship Invitational Barbecue

Fat Boys' Barbecue Team, Temple, Texas · Though it has few ingredients, the Fat Boys' brisket packs a lot of flavor. The secret is in the seasoning mix and in the long, slow cooking time.

3 tablespoons Harley's Texas-Style Seasoning (white label)

1 tablespoon granulated garlic

½ teaspoon coarsely ground black pepper

One 10- to 12-pound beef brisket (do not trim fat)

✪ In a small bowl, mix together the seasoning, garlic and pepper.

✪ Briefly rinse the brisket under cold running water and rub both sides generously with the seasoning mixture. Place the seasoned brisket in a 2-gallon heavy-duty locking plastic bag and seal the bag well. Place the brisket in the refrigerator for 8 to 10 hours.

✪ Build a fire in the firebox of a barbecue pit, using oak or pecan wood if available, and let the fire burn for about 45 minutes.

✪ Place the brisket on the grill grid, fat-side up, at the opposite end from the fire. Cook the brisket, undisturbed, for about 4 to 5 hours; the fire should remain at a temperature between 275 and 300 degrees.

✪ Wrap the brisket tightly in foil and cook for 3 to 4 more hours, keeping the temperature around 300 degrees.

✪ Cool the brisket and slice against the grain to serve.

SERVES 16 TO 20

Southern Greens with Pot Liquor

Jack Daniel's World Championship Invitational Barbecue

Reprinted from "Jack Daniel's The Spirit of Tennessee Cookbook" (Rutledge Hill Press): Lynne Tolley and Pat Mitchamore · Pot liquor is the broth that is left behind after the cooked greens are removed from the pan. Died-in-the-wool Southerner's use cornbread to sop it up.

1 ham hock, or 4 strips bacon, or 2 ounces diced salt pork

2 cups water, or more if necessary

1 pound turnip greens, mustard greens, collard greens or kale

1/2 teaspoon red pepper flakes

Salt and freshly ground pepper to taste

✪ If using the ham hock, place the ham hock in a saucepan with the water and bring to a boil. Reduce the heat to low and simmer until tender. Add more water if needed to keep it at 2 cups.

✪ If using the bacon or salt pork, sauté in a heavy saucepan until crisp. Remove from the heat and add the water to the pan.

✪ Carefully wash the greens and remove the tough stems and blemished parts. Add the greens to the pot with the liquid. Add the pepper flakes.

✪ Simmer the greens, covered, for 25 to 30 minutes, or until tender. Season with salt and pepper.

✪ If using the ham hock, remove it from the pot. Remove and discard the skin and fat. Remove the meat from the bone, tear the meat into bite-sized pieces and return them to the pot; discard the bone.

✪ Serve immediately.

SERVES 4 TO 6

ONION AND APPLE BAKE

Jack Daniel's World Championship Invitational Barbecue

Reprinted from "Jack Daniel's The Spirit of Tennessee Cookbook" (Rutledge Hill Press): Lynne Tolley and Pat Mitchamore · This simple side dish is the perfect companion to roast pork.

2 large onions, sliced

2 medium apples, peeled, cored and sliced

4 slices bacon, cooked until crisp and crumbled

1 tablespoon bacon drippings

1/3 cup soft bread crumbs

1/2 cup chicken stock

✪ Preheat the oven to 350 degrees. Grease an 8-inch square baking dish.

✪ Layer the onion slices, apple slices and bacon in the dish.

✪ In a skillet, heat the bacon drippings over medium heat until liquefied. Add the bread crumbs and stir until the bacon fat is absorbed; set aside.

✪ Pour the chicken stock over the casserole and bake, covered, for 30 minutes.

✪ Top the casserole with the bread crumbs and bake, uncovered, for 15 minutes, until the top is golden.

SERVES 2 TO 3

CARAMEL-PECAN CHEESECAKE

Jack Daniel's World Championship Invitational Barbecue

First Place, Dessert Category: Fat Boys' Barbecue, Temple, Texas · Serve this impressive dessert for a company dinner or family get-together. You can do most of the prep ahead of time and assemble it at the last minute. Take care not to bake the cake too long, or it could fall.

CRUST

2 cups Pecan Sandies shortbread cookie crumbs (about 15 cookies)

2 tablespoons butter or margarine, melted

2 tablespoons sugar

FILLING

Three 8-ounce packages cream cheese, at room temperature

1 cup firmly packed light brown sugar

2 tablespoons all-purpose flour

4 eggs

1/2 cup sour cream

1 teaspoon vanilla extract

1/4 teaspoon salt

TOPPING

1/2 cup sweetened condensed milk

1/3 cup light corn syrup

1/4 cup granulated sugar

3 tablespoons firmly packed brown sugar

3 tablespoons butter or margarine

1 tablespoon heavy cream

1/2 teaspoon vanilla extract

1/3 cup chopped toasted pecans

1/4 to 1/2 cup pecan halves

✪ For the crust, combine the cookie crumbs, melted butter or margarine and sugar in a bowl and mix well. Press the crumb mixture into the bottom of an ungreased 9- or 9 1/2-inch spring-form pan. Cover and chill for 30 minutes.

✪ Preheat the oven to 325 degrees.

✪ For the filling, place the cream cheese in a large bowl and beat with an electric mixer until fluffy. Add the brown sugar and flour and beat until well mixed. Add the eggs, one at a time, beating well after each addition. Add the sour cream, vanilla and salt and beat well. Pour the filling into the chilled crust and spread evenly.

✪ Bake the cheesecake for 55 to 65 minutes, or until the center is almost set, checking frequently. Turn off the oven and open the door partially. Leave the cake in the oven for 1 hour; remove the cake from the oven and cool completely on a wire rack. Carefully wrap the cooled cake and chill for at least 4 hours.

✪ For the topping, combine the sweetened condensed milk, corn syrup and sugars in a heavy medium saucepan. Heat the ingredients over medium heat, stirring constantly, until the mixture reads 220 degrees on a candy thermometer (check to see that the thermometer does not touch the bottom of the pan). Remove the mixture from the heat and stir in the butter, cream and vanilla extract. Let stand for 30 minutes to cool.

✪ To serve the cheesecake, remove the sides of the springform pan. Press the chopped pecans into the sides of the cake and place on a serving plate. Slowly pour the topping onto the cake until it is 1/2 inch from the edge. With a hot, wet knife, cut the cheesecake into serving pieces and garnish each piece decoratively with the pecan halves. Serve the cheesecake with the remaining topping on the side as a sauce.

SERVES 16

CHICKEN JAMBALAYA

Gonzales Jambalaya Festival

*1998 Champion and Three-Time World Champion: Byron Gautreau, Gonzales, Louisiana ·
Serve Byron's world-champion recipe in the traditional manner, accompanied by white beans,
a green salad and slices of French bread.*

½ cup vegetable oil

One 4- to 5-pound chicken

2 teaspoons freshly ground black pepper

3 medium onions, chopped

2 teaspoons garlic powder

8 cups water

2 tablespoons salt

½ teaspoon Accent seasoning (optional)

¼ teaspoon cayenne pepper

1 teaspoon Tabasco sauce

4 cups long-grain rice (uncooked)

✪ In a heavy pot, heat the oil over high heat. Season the chicken with the pepper and place in the hot oil. Brown the chicken on all sides, reducing the heat to medium if it is browning too quickly.

✪ Add the onions and 1 teaspoon of the garlic powder and sauté over low heat until the onions turn translucent.

✪ Add the water, stir, and bring the mixture to a full boil. Remove the pot from the heat and allow the grease to rise to the surface. Skim off as much of the grease as possible, taking care not to remove much of the broth.

✪ Add the remaining 1 teaspoon garlic powder, salt, Accent, if using, cayenne and Tabasco and return to a boil. Adjust the seasonings to taste, allowing a little excess seasoning to account for the addition of the rice.

✪ Add the rice and bring to a full boil, stirring to prevent sticking. Reduce the heat to very low, cover and simmer for 10 minutes.

✪ Remove the lid and stir the mixture, pushing the rice down into the liquid. Replace the lid and cook for 20 minutes.

✪ Remove the lid, stir and serve immediately.

SERVES 8

VARIATION - Pork and Sausage Jambalaya: For the chicken, substitute 3 pounds boneless pork, cut into cubes and 1 pound link sausage, cut into 1-inch pieces.

SWEET POTATO CASSEROLE

Gonzales Jambalaya Festival

Reprinted from the St. Theresa of Avila School Cookbook: Irene Allbritton, Gonzales, Louisiana • Choose either yellow- or orange-fleshed sweet potatoes for Irene's casserole. Orange-fleshed sweet potatoes are sometimes labeled as yams in the supermarket.

3 cups mashed sweet potatoes, fresh or canned

1/2 cup granulated sugar

1/2 cup butter, melted

2 eggs, beaten

1 teaspoon vanilla extract

1/3 cup milk

TOPPING

1/2 cup butter

1 cup light brown sugar

1/2 cup flour

1 cup chopped pecans

✪ Preheat the oven to 350 degrees.

✪ Place the sweet potatoes in a large bowl with the granulated sugar, melted butter, eggs, vanilla and milk; stir until well blended. Transfer the mixture to a 9-x-13-inch baking dish.

✪ For the topping, melt the butter in a saucepan. Add the brown sugar, flour and pecans and mix well.

✪ Sprinkle the topping evenly over the casserole.

✪ Bake the casserole for 25 minutes, until hot throughout.

SERVES 10 TO 12

SIMMERED WHITE BEANS

Gonzales Jambalaya Festival

*Michael Latuso, Sr., Gonzales, Louisiana · According to the locals in Gonzales,
"the Jambalaya Capital of the World," the most popular side dish for jambalaya is white beans.
Michael favors Michigan navy beans for his recipe.*

1 pound dried white beans, picked over

6 to 8 cups cold water

2 large onions, chopped

1 medium-sized green bell pepper,
    chopped

5 cloves garlic, chopped

1 pound ham hocks or ham pieces

Salt and freshly ground black pepper
    to taste

✪ Soak the beans in cold water to cover for about 2 hours. Drain and rinse the beans.

✪ Place the beans in a heavy large pot with the 6 to 8 cups cold water. Add the onions, pepper, garlic and ham hocks and bring to a boil over high heat. Reduce the heat to low and simmer for 2 to 2¹/₂ hours, until the beans are soft.

✪ Season with salt and pepper.

SERVES 8 TO 10

CHOCOLATE CHIP PECAN BREAD PUDDING WITH WHISKEY CREAM

Chef Jake Southworth, Cook-Off America Kitchen · Don't throw away your bread when it goes stale—save it for bread pudding. Jake recommends leaving the crust on the bread for a chewy texture; removing the crust for a light texture.

1 large loaf French bread (about 1 to 1½ pounds), cut into cubes

1 cup sugar

2 cups milk

1½ cups heavy cream

4 eggs, slightly beaten

2 tablespoons vanilla extract, or 1 vanilla bean, scraped

2 tablespoons ground cinnamon

1 cup pecans

1 cup semisweet chocolate chips

WHISKEY CREAM

1 cup heavy cream

2 teaspoons vanilla extract

3 tablespoons confectioners' sugar

2 to 4 tablespoons bourbon

✪ Preheat the oven to 350 degrees. Butter or spray an 11-x-7-inch glass baking dish.

✪ Place the bread cubes into a large mixing bowl.

✪ In another bowl, combine the sugar, milk, cream, eggs, vanilla, cinnamon, pecans and chocolate chips and whisk well.

✪ Pour the egg mixture over the bread and let stand until well absorbed. Transfer the mixture to the prepared baking dish. Bake for 35 to 40 minutes, until a toothpick inserted into a bread cube comes out almost clean.

✪ For the whiskey cream, combine all ingredients in a bowl. With an electric mixer, beat the mixture for about 1 to 2 minutes, until light and fluffy. Serve with the warm bread pudding.

SERVES 6 TO 8

THREE LITTLE PIGS PORK BUTT

American Royal / K.C. Masterpiece International Invitational Barbecue Contest

Grand Champions: Three Little Pigs Barbecue Team • For the best flavor, the Three Little Pigs Team recommends using apple, hickory, pecan or a combination of the woods in your smoker. Serve this pork butt alone with your favorite barbecue sauce, or heaped on a bun as a sandwich. Top it with sliced dill pickles or coleslaw, or serve them on the side.

BARBECUE SEASONING

1 cup brown sugar

1/2 cup salt

1/4 cup celery salt

1/2 cup paprika

3 tablespoons chili powder

2 tablespoons freshly ground black pepper

1 tablespoon lemon pepper seasoning

1 teaspoon garlic powder

1/2 teaspoon ground cinnamon

1/4 teaspoon cayenne pepper

One 5- to 6-pound bone-in lean pork butt

Yellow mustard

Thick sliced bacon

Apple juice

K.C. Masterpiece Original barbecue sauce

✪ In a small bowl, mix the barbecue seasoning ingredients.

✪ Coat the pork butt with the mustard and sprinkle liberally with the barbecue seasoning. Pierce the meat with a fork in several places and lay several slices of bacon over the top. Place the coated pork butt in a heavy-duty locking plastic bag and seal the bag well. Refrigerate for at least 8 hours.

✪ Prepare a smoker using 75 percent charcoal and 25 percent wood. Remove the pork from the bag and place on the grill grid of the smoker. Cook the pork between 175 and 200 degrees for 10 hours.

✪ Fill a clean spray bottle with apple juice. While the pork is cooking, spray it with apple juice every hour to moisten.

✪ When the pork reaches an internal temperature of 160 degrees, increase the temperature of the smoker to 300 degrees. Continue to cook the pork for about 1 to 2 hours, until the bone slips easily from the meat. While the pork is smoking, spray it with apple juice every 30 minutes.

✪ Remove the pork from the smoker, cover loosely with foil and let cool until easy to handle.

✪ To serve, pull or shred the pork with your fingers into bite-sized pieces. Serve with barbecue sauce.

SERVES 8 TO 12

GRILLED BRATWURST

American Royal / K.C. Masterpiece International Invitational Barbecue Contest

First Place Winner, Sausage Category: Bill Ritter, The Mudcreek BBQ & Chili Co., Arlington, Texas • Tiger Sauce, a dark-colored sauce flavored with crushed red peppers, is available in the supermarket near the barbecue sauce or in the Asian food section. Port Arthur sweet and sour sauce can be found in the Asian food section. You can substitute another brand of sweet and sour sauce, if desired, but look for an orange-colored and slightly runny type of sauce.

8 to 10 Johnsonville Brats, or bratwursts of your choice

Two 12-ounce cans Coca-Cola

One 5-ounce bottle Tiger Sauce or Sunshine Sauce

One 5-ounce bottle Port Arthur Sweet and Sour sauce

Juice from $1/2$ lemon

Seasoning salt or dry barbecue rub

✪ Prepare a hot barbecue fire.

✪ Place the bratwursts in a heavy saucepan with the Coca Cola. Bring the mixture to a boil over high heat. Reduce the heat to low and simmer for 15 minutes.

✪ In a bowl, mix together the Tiger Sauce, sweet and sour sauce and lemon juice.

✪ Remove the brats from the cooking liquid and sprinkle lightly with seasoning salt or dry barbecue rub. Place the brats on the grill and brush with the sauce mixture. Cook until the brats are browned and have good grill marks. Serve warm.

SERVES 8 TO 10

GRILLED CHEESE POTATOES

American Royal / K.C. Masterpiece International Invitational Barbecue Contest

Reprinted from "The Kansas City Barbecue Society Cookbook": Darrell and Karen DeGreve · Here's an easy side dish for a barbecue party. Just throw the packet of potatoes, onions and cheese on the grill alongside the meat, poultry or fish. If you're serving a crowd, enclose additional portions of ingredients in separate foil pouches to be sure that the potatoes cook through.

1 to 2 teaspoons vegetable oil

8 red potatoes, unpeeled, cut into cubes

1 large red onion, finely chopped

$1/2$ cup butter, cut into cubes

$1/2$ cup shredded Swiss cheese

$1/4$ cup freshly grated Parmesan cheese

$1/2$ teaspoon garlic powder

Salt and freshly ground pepper to taste

✪ Prepare a hot barbecue fire.

✪ Brush a large sheet of heavy-duty aluminum foil with vegetable oil. Place the potatoes and onion in the center of the foil. Top with the butter, cheeses, garlic powder, salt and pepper and mix gently.

✪ Fold the foil into a packet and seal the edges well. Wrap in another piece of foil.

✪ Place the packet on the hot grill and cook for 25 minutes per side, until the potatoes are cooked through.

SERVES 4

BARBECUE BEANS

American Royal / K.C. Masterpiece International Invitational Barbecue Contest

*Grand Champions, Side Dish Competition: Hi-Tech Smokers Barbecue Team ·
When you're pressed for time, doctor-up canned baked beans and pop them into a low oven —
they cook while you prepare the rest of the meal.*

2 teaspoons Dijon-style mustard

³/₄ cup brown sugar

¹/₃ cup barbecue sauce

¹/₃ cup ketchup

¹/₂ onion, chopped

1 teaspoon molasses

1 tablespoon chili powder

¹/₈ teaspoon cayenne pepper, or more
   to taste

¹/₂ teaspoon Liquid Smoke

1 cup chopped smoked beef brisket

Three 15-ounce cans baked beans

✪ Preheat the oven to 200 degrees.

✪ In a large heavy ovenproof saucepan, combine the mustard, brown sugar, barbecue sauce, ketchup, onion, molasses, chili powder, cayenne, Liquid Smoke and brisket. Stir until well mixed and heat through.

✪ Add the beans and stir well. Cover the pan and place in the oven. Bake for 1 hour or until heated through and the flavors are blended. Serve warm.

SERVES 8 TO 12

OLD COUNTRY POTATO SALAD

American Royal / K.C. Masterpiece International Invitational Barbecue Contest

*Reprinted from "The Kansas City Barbecue Society Cookbook": Ginger Stephens ·
Ginger's take on classic potato and egg salad is flavored with two types of pickles, two types
of mustard and piquant green olives.*

6 medium potatoes, cooked, peeled and cut into cubes

5 hard-cooked eggs, chopped

2 large dill pickles, chopped

4 sweet pickles, chopped

1 medium-sized yellow onion, chopped

1/2 cup sliced green olives

1 1/2 cups mayonnaise-type salad dressing

2 tablespoons Dijon-style mustard

1 tablespoon yellow mustard

1 teaspoon lemon juice

1 teaspoon freshly ground black pepper

1 teaspoon dill weed

3 hard-cooked eggs, cut into wedges

Paprika

✪ In a large bowl, combine the potatoes, chopped eggs, dill pickles, sweet pickles, onion and olives and mix gently.

✪ In another bowl, combine the salad dressing, Dijon-style mustard, yellow mustard, lemon juice, pepper and dill and mix well.

✪ Add the salad dressing mixture to the potato mixture and mix well.

✪ Transfer the potato salad to a serving bowl and garnish with egg wedges. Sprinkle with paprika.

✪ Cover the bowl and chill until serving time.

SERVES 12

GRILLED CHICKEN

American Royal / K.C. Masterpiece International Invitational Barbecue Contest

First Place, Chicken Category: Lola Rice, The USA Smoke Barbecue Team · Veterans of cooking competitions, Jim and Lola Rice of the USA Smoke Barbecue Team travel the country promoting Texas-style barbecue. Here is a good example of their prize-winning cooking style.

RUB

3 tablespoons granulated garlic

3 tablespoons salt

3 tablespoons sugar

2 teaspoons freshly ground black pepper

2 teaspoons poultry seasoning

2 teaspoons onion powder

¼ cup Dijon-style mustard

4 teaspoons Worcestershire sauce

8 chicken breast halves with skin,
    rib bone removed

Barbecue sauce (optional)

✪ In a large locking plastic bag, combine the rub ingredients and shake to mix well.

✪ In a small bowl, combine the mustard and Worcestershire. Rub the mustard mixture over the chicken and place in the bag with the rub. Shake to coat the chicken with the rub. Seal the bag well and refrigerate overnight.

✪ Prepare a medium-hot barbecue fire.

✪ Remove the chicken from the bag and place on the grill. Grill for about 10 minutes per side, until cooked through. If desired, brush with your favorite barbecue sauce during the last few minutes of cooking.

SERVES 4 TO 8

Barbecued Texas Brisket

American Royal / K.C. Masterpiece International Invitational Barbecue Contest

Lola Rice, The USA Smoke Barbecue Team · Brisket is a cut of beef that comes from the "breast" of the steer. It's an inexpensive cut that requires long, slow cooking to make it tender.

¹/₂ cup mustard, any style

6 tablespoons Worcestershire sauce

One 7-pound flat-cut beef brisket

RUB

¹/₄ cup granulated garlic

¹/₄ cup salt

¹/₄ cup sugar

¹/₄ cup freshly ground black pepper

¹/₄ cup chili powder

1 teaspoon cayenne pepper

Barbecue sauce

✪ In a small bowl, combine the mustard and the Worcestershire. Rub the meat on all sides with the mustard mixture.

✪ In a large, heavy-duty locking plastic bag, combine the rub ingredients and shake until well mixed. Place the meat in the bag, seal the bag well and shake to coat the meat with the rub. Refrigerate overnight.

✪ Preheat a smoker to 200 degrees, following the manufacturer's instructions.

✪ Remove the meat from the bag and place on the smoker's grill grid. Cook the meat at 200 degrees for 4 to 5 hours, or until the internal temperature reaches 155 to 160 degrees.

✪ Wrap the meat with foil and cook until the internal temperature reaches 185 to 190 degrees.

✪ Remove the meat from the grill and cool for 1 hour.

✪ To serve, slice the meat against the grain and serve with barbecue sauce on the side.

SERVES 12

GRILLED BARBECUE-SPICED POTATOES

American Royal / K.C. Masterpiece International Invitational Barbecue Contest

The Hi-Tech Smokers Barbecue Team · The grill is not only good for cooking meat, but also vegetables. Sliced zucchini, eggplant and onions are good choices. Potatoes are too, especially when rubbed with the Hi-Tech Smokers' barbecue spice before grilling.

6 medium potatoes

SPICE RUB

1 tablespoon seasoned salt

1 tablespoon garlic powder

1 tablespoon sugar

1 tablespoon dried Italian herb seasoning

$1/2$ tablespoon freshly ground black pepper

$1/2$ tablespoon onion powder

$1/2$ tablespoon paprika

Canola oil

✪ Boil the potatoes in water until slightly underdone. Cool and cut into $1/2$-inch-thick slices.

✪ Prepare a medium-hot barbecue fire.

✪ In a bowl, mix the spice rub ingredients. Add enough canola oil to make a thin paste. Brush the mixture over the potatoes.

✪ Place the potatoes on the grill and cook, turning, until golden brown and cooked through.

SERVES 5 TO 6

Sauteed Vegetables

American Royal / K.C. Masterpiece International Invitational Barbecue Contest

The Hi-Tech Smokers Barbecue Team · Bacon adds a smoky hint to sautéed vegetables and is a perfect complement to grilled foods.

2 slices bacon

$1/2$ cup thinly sliced red bell pepper

$1/2$ cup thinly sliced yellow bell pepper

$1/2$ cup thinly sliced green bell pepper

$1/2$ cup thinly sliced mushrooms

$1/2$ cup thinly sliced celery

$1/2$ cup thinly sliced carrots

$1/2$ cup thinly sliced sweet onion

1 cup sliced zucchini

1 cup sliced yellow squash

Garlic salt to taste

Freshly ground black pepper to taste

Dried Italian herb seasoning to taste

✪ In a large skillet, cook the bacon until crisp. Remove the bacon from the pan and crumble; reserve the bacon fat.

✪ To the skillet, add the peppers, mushrooms, celery, carrots and onion and sauté for about 1 minute. Add the zucchini and yellow squash and sauté until tender-crisp.

✪ Season the vegetables with garlic salt, pepper and Italian herbs. Stir in the bacon. Serve immediately.

SERVES 8 TO 10

CHICKEN PICATTA

Goleta Lemon Festival

Courtesy of Epicure Catering, Ventura, California · Serve this version of chicken picatta anytime—it's suitable for both a weeknight family dinner or company get-together. Serve it with cooked pasta, if desired.

8 to 10 boneless skinless chicken breast halves

2 cups flour seasoned with salt and freshly ground black pepper

1/4 cup olive oil or clarified butter

1 cup minced onions

1 cup sliced mushrooms

3 tablespoons capers, rinsed

1/2 cup fresh lemon juice

1/2 teaspoon lemon pepper seasoning

2 tablespoons sugar

1/2 cup dry white wine

1 tablespoon cornstarch mixed with 1 1/2 tablespoons water

Chopped fresh parsley for garnish

✪ Place the chicken and seasoned flour in a large locking plastic bag. Seal the bag well and shake until the chicken is well coated.

✪ In a large skillet, heat the oil or butter over medium-high heat. Carefully place the chicken into the hot oil and cook until browned on both sides.

✪ Add the onions and mushrooms and cook for 1 to 2 minutes, until the mushrooms are tender. Add the capers, lemon juice, lemon pepper, sugar, wine and cornstarch mixture and cook until the chicken is cooked through and the sauce is thickened. Sprinkle with chopped parsley.

SERVES 8 TO 10

POTATO SOUP WITH MEYER LEMONS

Goleta Lemon Festival

Reprinted from "Citrus" (Chronicle Books): Ethel and Georgeanne Brennan • This soup can also be served cold. Cover and refrigerate the pureed soup until well chilled. Adjust the seasonings before ladling into chilled bowls. Serve with crunchy slices of garlic toast alongside. If you cannot find Meyer lemons, you can substitute regular lemons with a little added sugar.

2 tablespoons butter

2 yellow onions, thinly sliced

1 tablespoon finely grated lemon zest (from about 2 lemons)

$1/2$ teaspoon grated peeled fresh ginger

1 cup strained fresh Meyer lemon juice, or regular lemon juice

$1/2$ teaspoon sugar, if using regular lemon juice, mixed with the lemon juice

$1/2$ teaspoon salt

$1/2$ teaspoon freshly ground black pepper

4 cups water

4 large red potatoes, peeled, boiled until tender and coarsely chopped

2 tablespoons finely chopped fresh Italian parsley

✪ In a saucepan over medium heat, melt the butter. When it begins to foam, add the onions, lemon zest, and ginger and sauté until the onions are translucent, about 10 minutes.

✪ Add the lemon juice (with the sugar, if using) salt and pepper; continue to sauté for 2 to 3 minutes longer.

✪ Add the water, increase the heat to high and bring to a boil. Cover the pan, reduce the heat to medium and simmer until the broth is golden and the onions have almost disintegrated, about 30 minutes.

✪ Remove the soup from the heat and strain through a sieve into a clean container; discard the contents of the sieve.

✪ Working in batches, if necessary, combine the strained broth and the potatoes in a blender or food processor and puree until smooth. Transfer the puree to a clean saucepan and bring to a gentle boil.

✪ Ladle the soup into warmed soup bowls and garnish each serving with a little of the parsley.

SERVES 4

LEMON BUTTER COOKIES

Goleta Lemon Festival

Reprinted from "Citrus" (Chronicle Books): Ethel and Georgeanne Brennan · These simple cookies are made from a creamy lemon batter speckled throughout with vanilla bean flecks. Substitute tangerine, lime or orange zest for the lemon zest to change the color and flavor.

2/3 cup butter, at room temperature

2 tablespoons finely grated lemon zest (from about 4 lemons)

1/2 cup granulated sugar

1 egg

1 vanilla bean, or 1/2 teaspoon pure vanilla extract

2 1/4 cups all-purpose flour

1/4 cup confectioners' sugar for garnish

✪ In a mixing bowl, cream the butter with the back of a fork until it is smooth, about 5 minutes. Add the lemon zest and continue to blend until well mixed. Add the granulated sugar and mix until smooth, about 2 minutes longer. Add the egg and beat vigorously until a lemony-yellow batter forms, another 5 minutes.

✪ Split the vanilla bean in half lengthwise. Using the tip of a sharp knife, scrape the tiny vanilla seeds into the batter and then stir to distribute evenly.

✪ Slowly stir in 2 cups of the flour, and mix until the dough pulls away from the sides of the bowl, and a ball forms. Remove the dough from the bowl, flatten into a small disk, and wrap in plastic or foil wrap. Chill for 15 minutes.

✪ Preheat the oven to 375 degrees.

✪ Generously flour a work surface and a rolling pin with part of the remaining 1/4 cup flour. Roll out the dough into a 1/4-inch-thick sheet. Using a 2-inch round cookie cutter, cut out the cookies and transfer them to an ungreased baking sheet, about 3/4-inch apart. Gather up the scraps, apply more flour to the work surface and rolling pin, and roll them out. Continue to cut out cookies until no dough remains.

✪ Bake the cookies until a golden brown edge appears around each cookie, 7 or 8 minutes. Remove from the oven and transfer to a wire rack. Let cool completely, about 30 minutes, then lightly dust with confectioners' sugar. Store in an airtight container at room temperature for up to 1 week.

MAKES ABOUT 3 DOZEN COOKIES

GOLETA LEMON FESTIVAL

a Valley Commerce

LEMON MERINGUE PIE

Goleta Lemon Festival

First Place: Vickie Mahan, Goleta, California · Since Vickie's pie uses raw eggs, it is important to bake it long enough that the meringue reaches 150 degrees, and is safe to eat. Spread the meringue in an even layer over the filling, taking care not to mound it in the center; this will ensure that the meringue bakes evenly.

$1/3$ cup plus 2 teaspoons cornstarch

2 cups sugar

$1/4$ teaspoon salt

$1^1/3$ cups water

4 egg yolks, slightly beaten

$1/3$ cup lemon juice

2 tablespoons grated fresh lemon zest

2 tablespoons butter or margarine

One 9-inch pie shell, baked (see NOTE)

4 egg whites, at room temperature

$1/4$ teaspoon cream of tartar

✪ In a small saucepan, combine the cornstarch, $1^1/2$ cups of the sugar and the salt. Gradually add the water, stirring until smooth. Cook over medium heat, stirring constantly, until it comes to a boil. Boil for 1 minute, stirring. Remove from the heat.

✪ Place the egg yolks in a medium bowl and gradually stir in half of the hot mixture, mixing well. Transfer the egg mixture to the saucepan and stir until well blended.

✪ Heat the mixture over medium heat until it comes to a rolling boil, stirring constantly; boil for 1 minute. Remove the mixture from the heat.

✪ Add the lemon juice, lemon zest and butter and immediately pour into the pie crust.

✪ Preheat the oven to 400 degrees.

✪ In a medium bowl, beat the egg whites with the cream of tartar until soft peaks form. While beating, gradually add the remaining $1/2$ cup sugar and continue to beat until stiff peaks form.

✪ Spread the mixture over the hot filling, spreading to the edge of the crust to seal the filling.

✪ Bake the pie for 7 to 9 minutes, or until the meringue is golden brown. Cool. Cut into wedges to serve.

MAKES ONE 9-INCH PIE

NOTE: To bake a pie shell, line with aluminum foil or parchment paper and fill with pie weights or dried beans. Place on the center oven rack and bake at 350 degrees for 20 minutes. Carefully remove the foil and the weights. Bake the pie shell for 10 to 15 more minutes, until firm. Cool completely before filling.

HOLY SMOKERS' RED BEANS & RICE

Memphis in May World Championship Barbecue Cooking Contest

Reprinted from the "Memphis in May International Festival Cookbook": Ernest E. Freeland, Jr. and Byron D. Ramsay, Jr., The Holy Smokers, Too BBQ Team • Andouille sausage is a spicy, smoked pork sausage popular in Cajun cooking.

1 pound dried red kidney beans

2 quarts cold water

2 medium onions

1/4 green bell pepper

1 cup chopped celery

4 dashes Tabasco sauce

3/4 teaspoon freshly ground black pepper

3/4 teaspoon cayenne pepper

3/4 teaspoon dried oregano

3/4 teaspoon dried thyme

1/2 teaspoon salt

1 small bay leaf

2 small cloves garlic

2 ham hocks

6 servings Minute Rice

1/4 pound smoked andouille sausage, cut into bite-sized pieces

Salt and freshly ground black pepper to taste

✪ Wash the beans and place them in a large saucepan with 1 quart of the water. Bring the mixture to a boil over high heat and boil for 2 minutes. Remove the pan from the heat, cover and let stand for 1 1/2 hours.

✪ Drain the beans and return them to the pan. Add the onions, green pepper, celery, Tabasco, black pepper, cayenne, oregano, thyme, salt, bay leaf, garlic cloves, ham hocks and remaining 1 quart water. Bring the mixture to a boil over high heat. Reduce the heat to low and simmer until tender.

✪ Remove the ham hocks from the pan. When cool enough to handle, remove the meat from the bone and cut into small pieces. Return the ham pieces to the pan with the beans and bring the mixture to a boil.

✪ Add the Minute Rice and sausage and simmer for about 10 minutes, adding more water if the mixture gets too thick.

✪ Let the mixture stand for 8 minutes before serving. Adjust the seasonings to taste.

SERVES 8

Super Swine Sizzlers' Pork Shoulder

Memphis in May World Championship Barbecue Cooking Contest

Reprinted from the "Memphis in May International Festival Cookbook": Jim Turner,
Super Swine Sizzlers BBQ Team · This award-winning pork shoulder is wonderful shredded
by hand, served on fresh sandwich buns, slathered with extra barbecue sauce and topped with
a mountain of coleslaw. The winning team prefers Wicker's brand Barbecue Sauce

DRY MIX POWDER

3 tablespoons paprika

1 tablespoon onion salt

1 tablespoon garlic salt

1 tablespoon ground basil

1$\frac{1}{2}$ tablespoons dry mustard

1 tablespoon cayenne pepper

$\frac{1}{2}$ tablespoon freshly ground black
    pepper

SUPER SWINE SIZZLERS' BARBECUE SAUCE

3$\frac{3}{4}$ cups purchased barbecue sauce

3$\frac{1}{2}$ tablespoons yellow mustard

3$\frac{1}{2}$ tablespoons lemon juice

3$\frac{1}{2}$ tablespoons beer

3 tablespoons Worcestershire sauce

3$\frac{1}{2}$ tablespoons butter

$\frac{1}{2}$ cup brown sugar

5 to 7 pounds pork shoulder

$\frac{1}{3}$ cup purchased barbecue sauce

$\frac{1}{3}$ cup cider vinegar

✪ For the dry mix powder, mix all ingredients together in a small bowl.

✪ For the sauce, mix all ingredients together until well blended. (Store the extras in a covered container.)

✪ Preheat a barbecue cooker to 250 to 300 degrees.

✪ Trim the excess fat from the pork shoulder. Rub the dry mix powder into the meat.

✪ Place the pork in the cooker and cook for 6 to 8 hours.

✪ While the meat is cooking, mix the $\frac{1}{3}$ cup purchased barbecue sauce with $\frac{1}{3}$ cup Super Swine Sizzlers' barbecue sauce and the $\frac{1}{3}$ cup cider vinegar; use the mixture to baste the meat lightly every 3 hours during cooking.

✪ Reduce the heat of the cooker to between 200 and 250 degrees and cook for 18 to 22 hours, until the meat is tender enough to be pulled apart easily.

✪ Serve the pork sliced or shredded with the remaining sauce as an accompaniment.

SERVES 8 TO 10

Bar-B-Q'd Pork Pizza

Reprinted from "John Willingham's World Champion Bar-B-Q"
(William Morrow and Company): John Willingham · Barbecued pork lends a rich, smoky flavor to
this Southern-style pizza. You may need to eat it with a knife and fork—it's a bit messy.

One 10-inch flour tortilla

¼ cup barbecue sauce

4 ounces barbecued pork shoulder, sliced

½ cup shredded mozzarella cheese

¼ cup freshly grated Parmesan cheese

Chopped red bell pepper for garnish (optional)

Chopped onion or green onions for garnish (optional)

Crumbled potato chips for garnish (optional)

✪ Preheat the oven to 350 degrees.

✪ Lay the tortilla on an ungreased baking sheet. Bake for 4 to 5 minutes, until crisp, turning once. Remove the tortilla, but do not turn off the oven.

✪ Heat the barbecue sauce in a small saucepan over medium heat until warm.

✪ Spread the pork in an even layer in a shallow microwave-safe dish. Microwave on high (100%) power for about 1 minute, or until hot.

✪ Brush a thin coat of barbecue sauce over the tortilla. Spread the pork evenly over the sauce and sprinkle the cheeses over the pork. Bake for about 2 minutes, until the cheeses melt.

✪ Cut the pizza into 8 wedges. Serve garnished with pepper, onions or green onions, and crumbled potato chips if desired.

SERVES 4

LAND O'COTTON HAWG COOKERS' BABY BACK RIBS

Memphis in May World Championship Barbecue Cooking Contest

Reprinted from the "Memphis in May International Festival Cookbook": Land O'Cotton Hawg Cookers • Flavor is added to these hearty pork ribs in three stages—with the dry rub before cooking, with the basting sauce while cooking and with the sweet sauce served with the ribs at the table.

DRY RUB

¹/₄ cup paprika

4 teaspoons freshly ground black pepper

2 teaspoons cayenne pepper

2 teaspoons dry mustard

4 teaspoons seasoned salt

4 teaspoons garlic powder

1 teaspoon dried oregano

1 teaspoon chili powder

SWEET SAUCE

¹/₂ cup butter

3 ounces tomato sauce

3 ounces sweet-hot mustard

1¹/₂ teaspoons brown sugar

1 cup ketchup

1 cup red wine vinegar

5 ounces Worcestershire sauce

1 teaspoon lemon juice

1 tablespoon paprika, or to taste

1 tablespoon seasoned salt, or to taste

1 teaspoons cayenne pepper, or to taste

¹/₂ teaspoon garlic powder, or to taste

BASTING SAUCE

1 cup red wine vinegar

¹/₄ cup brown sugar

¹/₂ teaspoon Louisiana hot pepper sauce

6 ounces beer

5 ounces Worcestershire sauce

¹/₂ bay leaf

2 slabs pork ribs

✪ For the dry rub, combine all ingredients in a small bowl and mix well.

✪ For the sweet sauce, mix all ingredients in a saucepan and bring to a boil. Reduce the heat to low and simmer for 30 minutes. Taste and adjust the spices. Cool completely and refrigerate until needed.

✪ For the basting sauce, mix all ingredients together, cover and refrigerate until needed.

✪ With your hands, rub the dry rub into the ribs.

✪ Heat a gas grill or barbecue cooker to low, about 190 to 220 degrees. Place the ribs bone-side down over indirect heat and cook for 4 to 6 hours, until the bone starts to separate from the meat. Baste the ribs with the basting sauce every 30 minutes. Serve the ribs with the sweet sauce.

SERVES 4 TO 8

HOT CABBAGE SLAW

Memphis in May World Championship Barbecue Cooking Contest

*Reprinted from the "Memphis in May International Festival Cookbook":
John D. Jeter, Pig Posse BBQ Team • Cayenne pepper adds punch to this version of coleslaw.
You can make it ahead of time and it will keep for several days before serving.*

1 firm head green cabbage, grated or
   sliced very thinly

1 medium onion, grated or sliced
   very thinly

½ green bell pepper, grated or sliced
   very thinly

1 cup sugar

1 cup white vinegar

1 tablespoon salt

1 teaspoon cayenne pepper

1 teaspoon paprika

1 teaspoon celery seeds

1 tablespoon freshly ground black pepper

✪ In a large bowl, mix the cabbage, onion and pepper until evenly mixed.

✪ In a bowl, whisk together the sugar, vinegar, salt, cayenne, paprika, celery seeds and pepper.

✪ Pour the dressing over the cabbage mixture and toss well. Cover and refrigerate the slaw overnight, or up to several days before serving.

SERVES 6 TO 8

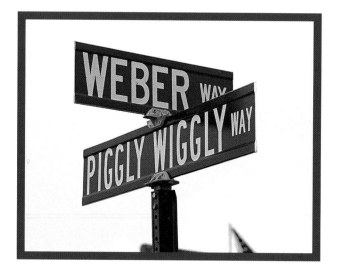

CHOCOLATE PRALINE JUMBO MUD SQUARES

Memphis in May World Championship Barbecue Cooking Contest

Reprinted from the "Memphis in May International Festival Cookbook":
Angela Hammond, Memphis in May Volunteer · So chocolatey they resemble the mud
in the Mississippi, these layered cookie bars make a perfect snack or casual dessert.

3/4 cup graham cracker crumbs

3/4 cup finely chopped pecans

1/4 cup firmly packed brown sugar

1/4 cup butter, melted

One 12-ounce jar caramel ice cream topping

3 tablespoons flour

1 cup butter

Four 1-ounce squares unsweetened baking chocolate

1 1/2 cups granulated sugar

1 cup flour

4 eggs, beaten

1 teaspoon vanilla extract

FROSTING

1 tablespoon butter

2 tablespoons unsweetened cocoa powder

1 to 2 tablespoons water

1 cup sifted confectioners' sugar

1/4 teaspoon vanilla extract

Confectioners' sugar for garnish (optional)

Pecans for garnish (optional)

Candied cherries for garnish (optional)

✪ Preheat the oven to 350 degrees.

✪ In a bowl, mix the graham cracker crumbs, pecans, brown sugar and melted butter. Press the mixture into the bottom of a greased 9-inch square pan. Bake the crust for 6 to 8 minutes; cool slightly.

✪ In a bowl, combine the caramel topping and the 3 tablespoons flour. Spread the mixture over the crust, leaving a 1/2-inch border; set aside.

✪ In the top of a double boiler, melt the 1 cup butter and the unsweetened chocolate. Add the granulated sugar, 1 cup flour, eggs and vanilla and mix well. Pour the mixture over the caramel mixture and spread evenly. Bake for 50 minutes and cool completely.

✪ While the dessert is cooling, make the frosting: combine the butter, cocoa and water in a small saucepan. Cook over medium heat until thickened. Stir in the 1 cup confectioners' sugar and vanilla extract. Spread the frosting over the cooled caramel mixture.

✪ Garnish the dessert with sifted confectioners' sugar, pecans and candied cherries, if desired.

SERVES 9 TO 12

MUSHROOM- AND HERB-STUFFED CHICKEN BREASTS

The Mushroom Festival

First Place, Junior's Category: Claire Shears, Kennett Square, Pennsylvania • Serve these easy-to-assemble stuffed chicken breasts over spinach fettuccine for a busy weeknight's meal.

FILLING

2 tablespoons extra-virgin olive oil

2 cloves garlic, minced

¾ cup sliced stemmed oyster mushrooms

¾ cup sliced stemmed shiitake mushrooms

¾ cup sliced cremini (brown) mushrooms

¼ cup chopped fresh parsley

½ cup chopped fresh basil

1 cup ricotta cheese

Salt and freshly ground black pepper
   to taste

16 ounces spinach fettuccine

6 tablespoons extra-virgin olive oil

4 boneless, skinless chicken breast halves,
   inside fillet attached

Salt and freshly ground black pepper
   to taste

½ cup dry white wine

1 cup heavy cream

✪ For the filling, heat the olive oil in a large skillet over medium-high heat. Add the garlic and sauté until golden; remove the garlic and discard.

✪ Add the mushrooms and cook for 5 to 7 minutes, until the mushroom liquid is released and then absorbed. Remove from the heat and stir in the parsley and basil.

✪ In a medium bowl, combine ½ cup of the mushroom mixture with the ricotta, salt and pepper and mix well.

✪ Cook the fettuccine according to package directions. Drain, toss with 2 tablespoons of the olive oil and keep warm.

✪ Lightly season the chicken breasts with salt and pepper.

✪ Holding each breast with the pointed end down, open a cavity behind the inside fillet with your fingers. Pack the filling into the cavity, taking care not to separate the fillet. Fold over the chicken breast and seal in the filling by pressing down along the edges with the side of a heavy knife.

✪ In a large skillet, heat the remaining ¼ cup olive oil over medium-high heat. Add the stuffed chicken breasts and cook for 3 to 4 minutes on each side, or until lightly browned and cooked through. Transfer the chicken to a warm platter and cover with foil.

✪ Add the wine to the skillet and stir with a whisk to dissolve the pan drippings. Stir in the remaining mushroom mixture and the cream. Cook over medium-high heat for 3 minutes, or until the sauce thickens. Correct the seasonings.

✪ Divide the cooked fettuccine among 4 heated dinner plates and top with the chicken breasts. Top with the mushroom sauce and serve immediately.

SERVES 4

MARINATED DUCK BREASTS WITH EXOTIC MUSHROOM TIMBALE, SPAGHETTI SQUASH AND FALL FRUIT COMPOTE

The Mushroom Festival

First Place, Professional Chef's Category: Gerald Schreck, Chef, The Terrace Restaurant, Kennett Square, Pennsylvania · The word "timbale" can refer to either a mold in which food is baked, or the dish that is baked into the mold. Demi-glace is a meat-based glaze that can be found in plastic containers in specialty food stores. Diluted, it serves as a lovely, rich sauce.

One spaghetti squash, about 3 pounds

FALL FRUIT COMPOTE

2 tablespoons unsalted butter

1 cup thinly sliced onions

3/4 cup chopped mixed red and yellow bell peppers

1/2 cup chopped dried apples

1/2 cup chopped dried pears

1/4 cup dried cranberries

1/4 cup golden raisins

1/2 cup packed brown sugar

1/2 cup raspberry vinegar

DUCK

2 tablespoons extra-virgin olive oil

1/4 cup dry white wine

1 tablespoon minced garlic

1 tablespoon chopped fresh parsley

1 tablespoon chopped fresh thyme

1 tablespoon chopped fresh rosemary

Two 10-ounce duck breasts

✪ Preheat the oven to 400 degrees.

✪ Cut the squash in half lengthwise and place cut-side down on an oiled baking sheet. Bake for 30 minutes. Remove the squash from the oven, cover with foil and set aside. Reduce the oven heat to 350 degrees.

✪ For the compote, melt the butter over medium heat in an ovenproof skillet. Add the onions and peppers and sauté for about 10 minutes, until soft.

✪ Add the dried fruit, brown sugar and vinegar and mix well. Remove from the heat. Cover the skillet and bake for 30 minutes, until syrupy. Remove from the oven and set aside.

✪ For the duck, combine the oil, wine, garlic, parsley, thyme and rosemary in a locking plastic storage bag and mix well. Add the duck breasts and seal the bag well. Let stand for 15 minutes.

✪ For the mushroom timbale, heat 2 tablespoons of the butter in a large skillet over medium-high heat. Add the shallots and garlic and sauté for 3 minutes, until transparent.

✪ Increase the heat to high. Add the mushrooms and sauté for 5 minutes. Stir in the herbs, salt and pepper and set aside.

✪ With the remaining 2 tablespoons butter, grease 4 large custard cups.

(recipe continued on next page)

Marinated Duck Breasts with Exotic Mushroom Timbale, Spaghetti Squash and Fall Fruit Compote
(CONTINUED)

MUSHROOM TIMBALE

1/4 cup butter

2 tablespoons minced shallots

1 tablespoon minced garlic

2/3 cup sliced cremini (brown) mushrooms

2/3 cup enoki mushrooms

2/3 cup sliced stemmed shiitake mushrooms

2/3 cup sliced stemmed oyster mushrooms

2 tablespoons chopped mixed fresh
    thyme, rosemary, parsley and chives

Salt and freshly ground black pepper
    to taste

16 sheets phyllo dough

1/2 cup demi-glace

1/2 cup dried cranberries for garnish

4 sprigs rosemary for garnish

✪ Press 4 sheets of phyllo into each custard cup, overlapping the sides. Working quickly, divide the mushroom mixture among the cups. Fold the overlapping phyllo over the mushroom mixture so that it is totally enclosed.

✪ Bake the timbales at 350 degrees for 15 minutes, or until lightly browned. Remove from the oven and keep warm.

✪ Remove the duck breasts from the marinade and pat dry with paper towels. Grill or broil the duck breasts over high heat for 3 minutes on each side; do not overcook. Remove from the heat and keep warm.

✪ In a small saucepan, dissolve the demi-glace in enough water to achieve a sauce consistency. Bring to a boil, whisking constantly. Remove from the heat, cover and keep warm.

✪ To serve, scrape the strands of the spaghetti squash onto the center of 4 heated serving plates using a large fork. Invert the mushroom timbales onto the squash and remove the molds.

✪ Slice the duck breasts thinly across the grain. Fan the slices out and lean them against the mushroom timbales on top of the squash; divide the slices evenly among the plates.

✪ Spoon the demi-glace over the duck breasts.

✪ Place a spoonful of fall fruit compote on each of the plates and garnish with dried cranberries and rosemary sprigs.

SERVES 4

MUSHROOM NAPOLEON

The Mushroom Festival

First Place, Cyber Category: Warren Mitchell Katz, Brooklyn, New York • Traditionally, the word Napoleon refers to a dessert consisting of a creamy filling sandwiched between layers of crisp pastry. Today, chefs are using the term Napoleon liberally, extending it to any number of sweet and savory concoctions. Warren's prize-winning dish is a good example.

2 pounds assorted mushrooms, such as white, cremini, shiitake and chanterelle

MUSHROOM SAUCE

1 small onion, chopped

2 cloves garlic, chopped

2 stalks celery, chopped

1/2 carrot, sliced

1 tablespoon fresh thyme leaves

2 cups vegetable stock

2 cups water

1/2 cup heavy cream

2 tablespoons cornstarch

Salt and freshly ground black pepper to taste

PASTRY LAYERS

8 sheets phyllo dough

6 tablespoons butter, melted

2 tablespoons chopped fresh thyme

FILLING

1/4 cup extra-virgin olive oil

2 cloves garlic, minced

1/4 cup brandy

3 tablespoons minced fresh parsley

Salt and freshly ground black pepper to taste

✪ Wipe the mushrooms clean with a damp cloth. Separate the mushroom stems from the mushroom caps.

✪ For the sauce, combine the mushroom stems, onion, garlic, celery, carrot, thyme, stock and water in a medium stockpot. Bring to a boil over high heat. Reduce the heat to low, partially cover the pot and simmer the stock for 40 minutes.

✪ Strain the stock and discard the solids. Return the liquid to stockpot and simmer until it is reduced to 2 cups.

✪ In a small bowl, combine the cream with the cornstarch and mix well. Whisk the cornstarch mixture into the simmering stock until slightly thickened. Season the sauce with salt and pepper and keep warm.

✪ For the pastry layers, preheat the oven to 350 degrees.

✪ Place the phyllo dough on a work surface and cover with plastic wrap and a damp cloth (this prevents the phyllo from drying out).

✪ In a small bowl, combine the butter and thyme.

✪ Place 1 sheet of the phyllo dough on a work surface and brush with the butter mixture. Top with another sheet of phyllo dough and brush with butter. Repeat the stacking and brushing process 2 more times; you should have 4 layers of phyllo dough.

✪ Trim the uneven edges of the phyllo and cut it into twelve 4-inch squares.

(recipe continued on next page)

MUSHROOM NAPOLEON
(CONTINUED)

✪ Transfer the phyllo squares to a parchment-lined baking sheet, cover with another sheet of parchment and place another baking sheet on top, pressing down securely. Bake the phyllo for 12 to 15 minutes, or until golden brown.

✪ Repeat with the remaining phyllo and butter mixture; you should have 24 phyllo squares.

✪ For the filling, heat the olive oil in a large skillet over medium heat. Add the garlic and mushroom caps (in batches if necessary) and sauté for 3 to 5 minutes.

✪ Add the brandy, parsley, salt and pepper and cook over high heat, stirring constantly, until the liquid evaporates; keep warm.

✪ To assemble the dish, spoon the mushroom sauce into a pool on each of 6 heated plates. Arrange 2 phyllo squares slightly askew on top of the sauce on each plate. Top the squares with the mushroom filling, dividing evenly. Top with 2 additional phyllo squares.

SERVES 6

RESPLENDENT STUFFED MUSHROOMS

The Mushroom Festival

Second Place, Cyber Category: Francis Benthin, Scio, Oregon · Francis's elegant appetizer is deceivingly easy to make. Look for mascarpone cheese, a rich Italian double-cream cheese, in a specialty food store or Italian market.

12 large white mushrooms

1 pound button mushrooms, sliced

¼ cup extra-virgin olive oil

2 tablespoons minced garlic

¼ cup finely chopped fresh parsley

Salt and freshly ground black pepper to taste

2 tablespoons chopped fresh rosemary

¼ cup minced roasted red bell pepper

⅔ cup dry white wine

½ cup mascarpone cheese

1½ cups Gorgonzola cheese

Rosemary sprigs for garnish

Roasted red pepper strips for garnish

✪ Preheat the oven to 350 degrees.

✪ Wipe all mushrooms clean with a damp cloth. Remove the stems from the large mushrooms, slice the stems and set aside. Place the mushroom caps gill-side up in a well-oiled baking pan.

✪ Mix together 2 tablespoons of the olive oil, 1 tablespoon of the minced garlic, the parsley, salt and pepper. Divide the mixture among the mushroom caps and bake for 10 minutes.

✪ Slice the button mushrooms and combine with the reserved mushroom stems.

✪ In a large skillet over medium-high heat, heat the remaining 2 tablespoons of the olive oil. Add the button mushrooms, remaining 1 tablespoon garlic and the rosemary and sauté for 3 minutes, until the mushrooms are limp.

✪ Add the red pepper and wine and sauté over high heat, stirring constantly, until most of the liquid has evaporated.

✪ Remove the mixture from the heat, stir in the cheeses and correct the seasonings.

✪ Divide the mushroom-cheese mixture among the baked caps. Bake for 5 additional minutes, until heated through.

✪ Place the mushroom caps on a serving plate and garnish with rosemary sprigs and roasted pepper strips.

SERVES 6

EASY MUSHROOM BRUNCH BAKE

The Mushroom Festival

First Place, Amateur Category: Terry Ann Moore · This mushroom-infused savory bread pudding is a perfect pick for an impromptu brunch.

6 slices white bread, crusts removed

8 ounces breakfast sausage, cooked and crumbled

1/4 cup diced onion

3 cups sliced mushrooms

6 eggs

1 cup Bisquick baking mix

2 cups milk

2 tablespoons Hellmann's Dijonnaise

2 tablespoons chopped fresh parsley

1/2 teaspoon dried sage

1 1/2 cups shredded cheddar cheese

Chopped green onions for garnish (optional)

✪ Preheat the oven to 350 degrees. Grease a 9-inch square glass pan.

✪ Line the prepared pan with the bread.

✪ In a bowl, mix the sausage, onion and mushrooms and add them to the pan with the bread.

✪ In another bowl, beat the eggs with the Bisquick, milk, Dijonnaise, parsley, sage and cheddar cheese. Pour the mixture into the pan.

✪ Bake the casserole for 45 to 50 minutes, or until puffed and golden brown.

✪ Cut the casserole into squares to serve. Garnish with green onions, if desired.

SERVES 9

VEGETABLE RISOTTO CAKES WITH MUSHROOMS

The Mushroom Festival

Winner, Professional Chef's Category: Peter Baxley, Chef, The City Club, Wilmington, North Carolina · Though Peter's recipe has several steps, some can be done in advance. The wild mushrooms can by pricy, so reserve this recipe for a special occasion.

1 cup oyster mushrooms

1 cup chanterelle mushrooms

RISOTTO CAKES

6 cups chicken stock

1/2 cup olive oil

1 medium onion, finely chopped

1 clove garlic, minced

1/4 cup finely diced carrot

1/4 cup finely diced celery

1 cup Arborio rice

1 cup dry white wine

1/2 cup freshly grated Parmesan cheese

SAUCE

8 cups vegetable stock

2 cups chopped tomatoes

1 cup balsamic vinegar

2 teaspoons sugar

Salt and freshly ground black pepper
  to taste

✪ Wipe the mushrooms clean with a damp cloth. Separate the mushroom stems from the caps. Chop the mushroom stems; slice the mushroom caps. Set the stems and caps aside separately.

✪ For the risotto cakes, bring the chicken stock to a boil in a medium saucepan over high heat. Reduce the heat to low and keep the stock at a simmer.

✪ In another medium saucepan, heat 1/4 cup of the olive oil over medium heat. Add the onion and sauté until translucent.

✪ Add the garlic, carrot and celery and sauté for about 3 minutes, until softened.

✪ Add the rice and stir to coat the rice grains with oil. Add the wine and cook, stirring constantly, until the wine has evaporated.

✪ Stir in 1 or 2 ladlesful of the simmering stock, enough to coat the rice. Cook, stirring constantly, over medium heat until the stock has been absorbed. Continue cooking and stirring the rice, adding the stock a little at a time for about 20 minutes, or until the rice is cooked, but still slightly firm to the bite (al dente). Remove the pan from the heat and stir in the cheese.

✪ Pour the risotto into a 10-inch springform pan and cool. When cool, remove sides of the pan to release the risotto cake. With a 3-inch round cutter, cut the large risotto cake into 6 small risotto cakes.

¼ cup extra-virgin olive oil

2 cloves garlic, minced

1 small shallot, minced

2 tablespoons fresh thyme leaves

2 tablespoons chopped fresh basil

4 cups mixed baby field greens

Salt and freshly ground black pepper
to taste

White truffle oil

Basil tops for garnish

✪ In a large skillet, heat the remaining ¼ cup of the olive oil over medium-high heat. Quickly brown the risotto cakes on each side. Remove from the pan and keep warm.

✪ For the sauce, combine the vegetable stock, tomatoes, reserved mushroom stems, balsamic vinegar and sugar in a large stockpot. Bring the mixture to a boil over high heat. Reduce the heat to low and simmer, uncovered, for 45 minutes. Season with salt and pepper.

✪ In a large skillet, heat the olive oil over medium heat. Add the garlic and shallot and sauté until translucent. Add the reserved chopped mushrooms, thyme and basil and sauté for about 5 minutes, until the mushrooms are tender. Add the greens and stir until wilted. Season with salt and pepper.

✪ To assemble, place 1 risotto cake each in the center of 6 warmed serving plates. Spoon the sautéed mushrooms around the risotto cakes, dividing evenly. Spoon the sauce over the risotto cakes, drizzle with white truffle oil and garnish with basil.

SERVES 6

Onion-Parmesan Focaccia

North American Olive Oil Association's Olive Oil Everyday Recipe Contest

Runner-up, Appetizer Category: Courtesy of the North American Olive Oil Association • Serve this bread alone as a snack, or as an accompaniment to a meal of hearty soup or salad.

DOUGH

1 package active dry yeast

1⅓ to 1¾ cups spring water, heated for 10 seconds in a microwave on high (100%) power

¼ cup extra-virgin olive oil, plus more for oiling bowl and baking sheet

1½ tablespoons fine-grained sea salt or kosher salt

4 to 5 cups unbleached white flour

TOPPING

2 tablespoons extra-virgin olive oil

2 large onions, chopped

1 teaspoon dried oregano

1 teaspoon dried basil

5 ounces Parmesan cheese, grated

4 to 5 fresh plum tomatoes, sliced

✪ For the dough, mix the yeast and water in the bowl of a heavy duty mixer until dissolved. Add the olive oil, salt and flour. With the dough hook, knead the dough for 15 minutes.

✪ Form the dough into a ball and transfer to a large oiled bowl, turning to coat all sides of the dough with oil. Cover the bowl with plastic wrap and let the dough rise for 1 to 2 hours, until doubled in size.

✪ With your fingers, spread the dough slowly and evenly to the edges of an oiled baking sheet. Push the dough edges together slightly to form a crust. Cover the dough with plastic wrap and let rise for about 2 hours, until doubled in size.

✪ While the dough is rising, make the topping: In a skillet, heat the olive oil over medium heat. Add the onions, oregano and basil and sauté until the onions are soft; cool.

✪ Thirty minutes before the dough is risen, preheat the oven to 425 degrees.

✪ Spread the onion mixture evenly over the risen dough. Sprinkle with the Parmesan cheese and top with the tomatoes.

✪ Bake the focaccia on the center oven rack for 35 to 40 minutes, until golden brown and cooked through.

SERVES 12

ROASTED RED PEPPER AND SUN-DRIED TOMATO SPREAD

North American Olive Oil Association's Olive Oil Everyday Recipe Contest

Winner, Appetizer Category: Courtesy of the North American Olive Oil Association · You can use freshly prepared roasted red peppers, but remember to peel and seed them first. If you choose roasted peppers from a jar, drain them well before chopping. The sun-dried tomatoes should be rehydrated if dried, or drained well if packed in oil. In addition to coating flatbread, hearty crackers or melba toast, this spread doubles as a dip for vegetables or a sauce for pasta or risotto.

1 cup coarsely chopped roasted red
   bell peppers

3 tablespoons olive oil

1 clove garlic, smashed

8 medium-sized fresh basil leaves,
   thinly sliced

Red pepper flakes to taste

1 cup sun-dried tomatoes

Crackers, flatbread or melba toast
   as accompaniments

✪ In a food processor, combine the roasted peppers, olive oil, garlic, basil, red pepper flakes and sun-dried tomatoes and process until the desired consistency is reached.

✪ Transfer the spread to a serving bowl and serve with crackers, flatbread or melba toast.

SERVES 6 TO 10

FORK-TENDER STUFFED PORK ROAST

North American Olive Oil Association's Olive Oil Everyday Recipe Contest

*Winner, Entrée Category: Courtesy of the North American Olive Oil Association ·
This prize-winning entrée consists of a succulent pork roast filled with a savory stuffing
of apples, onions, mushrooms and Parmesan cheese.*

¾ cup plus 2 tablespoons extra-virgin olive oil

½ large Granny Smith apple, diced

1 medium-sized yellow onion, diced

2 to 3 cloves garlic, minced

1 pint white mushrooms, cleaned, stems removed, and chopped

About 2½ cups Italian-seasoned bread crumbs

¼ cup freshly grated Romano or Parmesan cheese

Salt and freshly ground black pepper to taste

One 4-pound boneless pork roast, fat trimmed

✪ Preheat the oven to 350 degrees.

✪ In a large nonstick skillet, heat the 2 tablespoons olive oil over medium-high heat. Add the apple and sauté until soft and slightly golden. Add the onion and garlic and sauté until the onion is transparent. Transfer the apple-onion mixture to a plate.

✪ Add the mushrooms to the skillet and sauté until slightly golden; remove and discard the juices from the mushrooms as they are released.

✪ Transfer the apple-onion mixture back to the skillet and stir until heated through.

✪ Add the ¾ cup olive oil to the skillet, then stir in the bread crumbs; remove from the heat. The mixture should be crumbly but not dry or oily; add a small amount of bread crumbs or olive oil if necessary. Stir in the grated cheese and season with salt and pepper.

✪ With a long knife, slice the roast in half lengthwise almost all the way through and open the meat so that it lays flat; transfer the meat to a roasting pan.

✪ Place the stuffing mixture in the middle of the meat. If desired, tie the meat together with kitchen string; it will not close all the way. (If there is extra stuffing, place it on top of the meat during roasting to add flavor.)

✪ Cover the roasting pan with aluminum foil. Place the pan in the oven and roast for 2 hours. Remove the foil from the pan and cook for 20 to 30 minutes, until the pork is cooked through and the top is slightly brown.

SERVES 8

MEDITERRANEAN CHOCOLATE CAKE

North American Olive Oil Association's Olive Oil Everyday Recipe Contest

*Winner, Dessert Category: Courtesy of the North American Olive Oil Association ·
Serve this moist cake as an everyday dessert. "Light" olive oil is lighter in color and olive flavor
than regular or extra-virgin olive oil, making it a perfect choice for baking.*

CAKE

3/4 cup all-purpose flour

1/2 cup unsweetened cocoa powder

1/4 teaspoon baking soda

1/4 teaspoon ground cinnamon

4 eggs

1/4 teaspoon salt

1 cup sugar

2 teaspoons finely grated lemon zest

2/3 cup light olive oil

GLAZE

1 cup confectioners' sugar

2 tablespoons water

1/2 cup unsweetened cocoa powder

Pinch salt

1 tablespoon light olive oil

1 to 2 teaspoons water (optional)

✪ Preheat the oven to 350 degrees. Grease a 9-inch springform pan or 2-inch-deep round cake pan with light olive oil.

✪ For the cake, combine the flour, cocoa, baking soda and cinnamon in a medium bowl.

✪ In a large bowl, whisk the eggs with the salt. While whisking, gradually add the sugar and lemon zest.

✪ Sift the flour mixture over the egg mixture, gradually folding it in with a spatula until the mixture is smooth.

✪ Gradually add the light olive oil, folding with the spatula until the mixture is smooth. Pour the batter into the prepared pan.

✪ Bake the cake for 40 to 45 minutes, or until the center bounces back when pressed lightly with a finger.

✪ Cool the cake in the pan on a wire rack for 10 minutes. With a knife, loosen the cake from the sides of the pan and invert the cake onto a rack. Cool the cake completely before glazing.

✪ For the glaze, combine the confectioners' sugar and water in a saucepan and stir until smooth.

✪ In a small bowl, mix the cocoa and the salt. Sift the cocoa mixture over the sugar mixture and blend well. Add the light olive oil and stir until well mixed.

✪ Place the pan over medium heat and heat until the mixture is just warm to the touch, stirring constantly. Add 1 to 2 teaspoons water if necessary to thin the glaze.

✪ With a spoon, drizzle the glaze over the top of the cake and let stand for 10 minutes to set before cutting.

SERVES 10 TO 12

OYSTER CHEESECAKES WITH OYSTER SAUCE AND CAVIAR

National Oyster Cook-Off

Grand Prize Winner and Appetizer Category Winner: Dawn L. Brown, Baltimore, Maryland ·
Dawn's recipe uses oysters in both the cheesecakes and the sauce for a fantastic oyster-lover's treat.
Oyster liquor is the briny liquid that remains in the shell after the oysters are shucked.
When you buy oysters in bulk, they come packed in their liquor in plastic containers.

6 ounces cream cheese, softened

2 large eggs

$^1/_2$ shallot, minced

1 tablespoon chopped seeded tomato

1 small clove garlic, minced

$1^1/_2$ teaspoons fresh lemon juice

Dash cayenne pepper

Dash seafood seasoning

1 dozen small- to medium-sized Maryland
   select oysters, shucked, liquor reserved

Salt and freshly ground white pepper
   to taste

OYSTER SAUCE

3 tablespoons butter

3 tablespoons flour

1 pint heavy cream

1 pint Maryland select oysters with liquor,
   finely chopped

Salt and freshly ground white pepper
   to taste

1 teaspoon seafood seasoning

1 tablespoon dry sherry

Caviar for garnish

✪ Preheat the oven to 350 degrees. Lightly coat four $^2/_3$-cup soufflé dishes with butter.

✪ With an electric mixer, beat the cream cheese until fluffy. Add the eggs and beat well.

✪ Add the shallot, tomato, garlic, lemon juice, cayenne and seafood seasoning and stir until blended. Add the shucked oysters and stir until blended. Season with salt and pepper.

✪ Divide the cheesecake mixture among the soufflé dishes and bake for about 30 minutes, until the centers are set. Remove from the oven and cool slightly.

✪ For the oyster sauce, melt the butter in a saucepan. Add the flour and stir until smooth. Cook the butter-flour mixture, stirring for several minutes, but do not let it brown.

✪ Add the cream to the flour mixture and stir until smooth and well mixed.

✪ Add the chopped oysters with their liquor and season with salt, pepper and seafood seasoning, stirring until mixed. Cook the sauce over medium heat until thickened. Stir in the sherry just before serving.

✪ To serve, run a sharp knife around the edges of the soufflé dishes to loosen the cheesecakes. Invert the cheesecakes onto serving plates and spoon the oyster sauce over the top. Garnish with small spoonfuls of caviar.

SERVES 4

Oyster'n Fennel Chowder

National Oyster Cook-Off

Winner, Soup/Stew Category: Alex DeSantis, Bethlehem, Pennsylvania · Take special care when preparing Alex's lively and interesting chowder, as it can separate if not prepared properly or served immediately. Fennel fronds are the green feathery leaves on the tops of the fennel stalks. They can be treated just like any herb.

1 quart Maryland oysters with liquor

1/4 cup dry white wine

1 large bulb fennel, halved and sliced very thinly

1 medium onion, chopped

2 teaspoons olive oil

3 cups homemade chicken stock or low-sodium canned chicken broth

1 cup grated carrots

1/4 teaspoon dried thyme

1/8 teaspoon cayenne pepper, or more to taste

Salt and freshly ground black pepper to taste

1/2 cup evaporated milk

Chopped fennel fronds for garnish

✪ Drain the oysters, reserving the liquor. Place the oysters in a shallow dish with the white wine; toss to coat the oysters well and let stand until needed.

✪ In a Dutch oven or large saucepan, sauté the fennel and onion in the oil over medium heat until wilted, about 5 minutes.

✪ Add the chicken stock, carrots, thyme, cayenne pepper, salt and black pepper.

✪ Bring the mixture to a boil over high heat. Cover the pan, reduce the heat to low and simmer until the vegetables are tender, about 15 minutes.

✪ Add the evaporated milk and heat very gently for 3 to 4 minutes.

✪ Add the reserved oysters and wine and cook for about 3 minutes, just until the oysters' edges begin to curl; do not allow the mixture to boil.

✪ If the chowder is too thick, add a small amount of the reserved oyster liquor to thin it to the desired consistency.

✪ Garnish servings with fennel fronds.

SERVES 4 TO 6

SICILIAN OYSTER SALAD

National Oyster Cook-Off

Winner, Salad Category: Wolfgang H.M. Hanau, West Palm Beach, Florida • Look for fresh oysters already shucked in plastic containers at a good-quality fish market. Oysters are extremely perishable, so keep them in the refrigerator or on ice at all times while working with them. Wolfgang uses Italian-style polenta instead of bread crumbs to add a crisp coating to his fried oysters.

2 medium ears fresh corn

1/2 cup diced sweet onion

2 cups diced Roma tomatoes

2 tablespoons aged balsamic vinegar

1/8 teaspoon salt

1 tablespoon sugar

1/4 teaspoon red pepper flakes

1/4 cup small Sicilian nonpareille capers

1/4 cup extra-virgin olive oil

1/2 cup slivered fresh basil leaves

1 cup sliced fresh mozzarella cheese
   (buffalo mozzarella preferred)

2 bunches fresh arugula

FRIED OYSTERS

48 fresh Maryland oysters (shucked)

2 eggs, lightly beaten

1/4 cup finely chopped oil-cured green
   olives

2 cups instant polenta

1 teaspoon sugar

2 teaspoons salt

1 teaspoon freshly ground black pepper

2 teaspoons flour

Olive oil for frying (do not use extra virgin)

✪ With a sharp knife, remove the corn from the ears. Place the corn kernels in a large nonstick skillet with the onion and cook over medium-high heat until heated through. Remove from the heat and transfer to a large bowl with the tomatoes and stir well.

✪ In a small bowl, whisk together the vinegar, salt, sugar, pepper flakes, capers and olive oil. Add to the bowl with the tomatoes; add the basil leaves and sliced mozzarella and toss lightly.

✪ Line 4 serving plates with arugula leaves and top with the corn mixture, dividing evenly.

✪ For the fried oysters, drain the oysters and place them in a bowl with the eggs and chopped green olives.

✪ In another bowl, combine the polenta, sugar, salt, pepper and flour and mix well.

✪ In a large rimmed skillet, heat about 1 inch of olive oil over medium-high heat until hot but not smoking.

✪ Dip the oysters into the polenta mixture and place in the hot oil. Fry the coated oysters until golden brown and drain on paper towels.

✪ Place the hot fried oysters on top of the corn salad and serve immediately.

SERVES 4

SIZZLIN' SPICY SCAMPI PIZZA

Mama Mary's Gourmet Pizza Crusts Pizza Creations Contest

First Place Winner, Traditional Category, 1997: Gloria Bradley, Naperville, Illinois · Shrimp, three cheeses and lots of garlic form the topping for Gloria's innovative pizza.

3 tablespoons extra-virgin olive oil

2 cloves garlic, minced

10 ounces medium shrimp, peeled and deveined (uncooked)

1½ tablespoons fresh lemon juice

2 large plum tomatoes, seeded and chopped

¼ cup chopped leek or green onions (white and green parts)

2 tablespoons snipped fresh chives

Salt and freshly ground black pepper to taste

⅓ cup Boursin or cream cheese with garlic and herbs, softened

One 12-inch Mama Mary's Gourmet Pizza Crust

¾ cup shredded mozzarella cheese

¼ cup freshly grated Parmesan cheese

2 teaspoons red pepper flakes

✪ Preheat the oven to 425 degrees.

✪ In a large nonstick skillet, heat 2 tablespoons of the oil over medium-high heat. Add the garlic and sauté for 30 seconds. Add the shrimp and sauté for 30 seconds. Add the lemon juice and cook briefly, until the shrimp are just underdone; set aside.

✪ In a medium bowl, mix the tomatoes, leek or green onions, and 1 tablespoon of the chives. Add the remaining 1 tablespoon oil and stir well. Season with salt and pepper.

✪ Spread the Boursin cheese evenly over the pizza crust. Top with the tomato mixture. Top with the shrimp.

✪ Sprinkle the pizza with the mozzarella and Parmesan cheeses and red pepper flakes.

✪ Bake the pizza for 10 to 12 minutes, until the cheese melts.

✪ Sprinkle the pizza with the remaining 1 tablespoon chives. Cut into wedges to serve.

SERVES 8

SMOKY THREE-CHEESE WHITE PIZZA

Mama Mary's Gourmet Pizza Crusts Pizza Creations Contest

*Second Place Winner, Traditional Category 1997: Patricia Schroedl, Jefferson, Wisconsin ·
Patricia's "white" pizza has no tomato sauce, but you won't miss it after sampling the topping
of smoky bacon and assertive blue cheese.*

8 slices bacon

1 tablespoon olive oil

1 large onion, thinly sliced

One 6-ounce jar marinated artichoke
  hearts, drained and chopped

One 12-inch Mama Mary's Gourmet
  Pizza Crust

4 ounces smoked Swiss cheese, sliced

1/2 cup sour cream

1/2 cup crumbled blue cheese

1/4 teaspoon garlic powder

1/4 cup freshly grated Asiago or
  Parmesan cheese

1 tablespoon chopped fresh Italian
  parsley

✪ Preheat the oven to 450 degrees.

✪ In a medium nonstick skillet, cook the bacon until crisp. Remove the bacon and drain on paper towels; discard the bacon grease. When cool enough to handle, crumble the bacon and set aside.

✪ In the same skillet, heat 1/2 tablespoon of the olive oil over medium heat. Add the onion and sauté until tender and lightly browned. Stir in the bacon and chopped artichokes and sauté until heated through; set aside.

✪ Brush the crust with the remaining 1/2 tablespoon olive oil. Arrange the Swiss cheese slices over the crust.

✪ In a small bowl, blend the sour cream, blue cheese and garlic powder. Spread the mixture over the Swiss cheese on the pizza crust. Top with the onion-artichoke mixture and sprinkle with the Asiago or Parmesan cheese.

✪ Place the pizza directly on the oven rack and reduce the oven temperature to 425 degrees. Bake the pizza for 10 to 12 minutes.

✪ Sprinkle the pizza with chopped parsley and cut into wedges to serve.

SERVES 8

APPLE STREUSEL DESSERT PIZZA

Mama Mary's Gourmet Pizza Crusts Pizza Creations Contest

First Place Winner, Dessert Category, 1997: Lori Hughes, Olathe Kansas • Pizza for dessert? Why not? Simply top a prepared pizza crust with sautéed apples and a buttery streusel topping and pop it in the oven. An easy icing drizzled over the top is the finishing touch.

STREUSEL TOPPING

$2/3$ cup sugar

$2/3$ cup flour

$1/2$ cup butter, at room temperature

2 apples, peeled and finely chopped

1 teaspoon ground cinnamon

$1/3$ cup sugar

One 12-inch Mama Mary's Gourmet
   Pizza Crust

2 tablespoons butter, softened

ICING

2 tablespoons butter, melted

2 tablespoons milk

1 cup confectioners' sugar

1 teaspoon vanilla extract

✪ Preheat the oven to 425 degrees.

✪ For the streusel topping, place the sugar and flour in a shallow bowl. Add the butter. With a pastry blender or 2 knives, cut in the butter until well combined and crumbly; refrigerate until ready to use.

✪ In a microwave-proof bowl, combine the apples, cinnamon and $1/3$ cup sugar. Mix well and microwave on high (100%) power for 2 minutes; set aside.

✪ Brush the pizza crust with the softened butter.

✪ Sprinkle the crust with $1/2$ of the streusel topping. Top with the apple mixture. Top with the remaining streusel topping.

✪ Place the pizza directly on the oven rack and bake for 8 to 10 minutes, until the topping is golden brown.

✪ While the pizza is baking, combine the icing ingredients in a small bowl and mix well.

✪ Drizzle the icing over the warm pizza. Cut the pizza into wedges to serve.

SERVES 8

BERRY CRUNCHY DESSERT PIZZA

Mama Mary's Gourmet Pizza Crusts Pizza Creations Contest

Second Place Winner, Dessert Category, 1997: Mary Cummings, New Smyrna Beach, Florida • Broken candy bars add the crunch to Mary's after-dinner treat, which is more like a fruit tart than a pizza.

3 tablespoons butter

2 teaspoons granulated sugar

1/2 teaspoon vanilla extract

One 12-inch Mama Mary's Gourmet Pizza Crust

1 tablespoon orange liqueur, such as Grand Marnier, Cointreau or Triple Sec

1/3 cup fruit-only strawberry or raspberry jam or preserves

1 cup pecans or walnuts, chopped

3 Heath chocolate-covered toffee candy bars, frozen (do not unwrap)

8 ounces regular or light cream cheese, at room temperature

1 cup sifted confectioners' sugar

1 cup sliced fresh strawberries

3/4 cup fresh red raspberries

3/4 cup fresh blueberries

Whipped cream for garnish

✪ Preheat the oven to 425 degrees.

✪ In a small saucepan or in the microwave, melt the butter. Add the sugar and vanilla and stir until the sugar is dissolved. Brush the mixture over the pizza crust.

✪ Bake the pizza crust directly on the oven rack for 8 to 10 minutes, watching carefully. Remove from the oven and cool on a wire rack.

✪ In a small bowl, combine the liqueur and the jam and stir well. Spread the jam mixture evenly over the crust, avoiding the rim. Sprinkle the jam with the nuts.

✪ With a wooden mallet, break the wrapped candy bars into bite-sized pieces. Unwrap the candy bars and sprinkle the candy pieces over the nuts.

✪ In a small bowl, mix the cream cheese and confectioners' sugar until smooth. Carefully spread the cream cheese mixture over the pizza.

✪ Transfer the pizza to a serving platter. Arrange the berries decoratively over the cheese mixture. Chill the pizza until serving time.

✪ Cut the pizza into wedges to serve and garnish servings with whipped cream.

SERVES 10

VERMONT FIESTA PAULKETS

Newman's Own / Good Housekeeping Recipe Contest

Grand Prize Winner, 1998: Diane Reilly, St. Albans, Vermont • Inspired by her family's prize-winning Holstein dairy cows, Diane and her fourth and fifth grade class used sour cream as a base in these delicious pockets, or "Paulkets." If the dough edges are not sealed properly, the filling may leak a bit, but they will still taste delicious.

Two 10-ounce packages refrigerated pizza dough

1/2 pound deli-style mesquite turkey breast, shaved

8 ounces Vermont mild cheddar cheese, shredded

One 11-ounce jar Newman's Own Medium Salsa

One 8-ounce container sour cream

✪ Preheat the oven to 425 degrees.

✪ On a floured work surface, unroll both packages of pizza dough and cut each into 4 squares.

✪ Arrange the turkey breast and cheese diagonally on half of each dough square, dividing evenly. Top with about 2 tablespoons each of salsa. Fold the empty half of the dough square over the filling. Fold the bottom dough edge up over the top edge and pinch to seal in the filling.

✪ Put the Paulkets on an ungreased baking sheet and bake for about 20 minutes, until the dough is cooked through and lightly browned.

✪ Serve with the remaining salsa and sour cream.

MAKES 8 PAULKETS

Rally 'Round the Ragout, Boys!

Newman's Own / Good Housekeeping Recipe Contest

Finalist, 1998: Marianne McGee, Madison, Alabama • Marianne created this sumptuous stew for her sister-in-law who is a gourmet cook. Keep a few prepared items on hand in the pantry and quick, elegant meals like this can be thrown together with little effort.

2 dried ancho chiles, stemmed and seeded

1/2 cup all-purpose flour

1 tablespoon dry mustard

1 tablespoon ground coriander

1 tablespoon freshly ground black pepper

3 to 3 1/2 pounds boneless pork shoulder or butt, cut into 1 1/2-inch cubes

1/4 cup olive oil

1/4 cup packed brown sugar

1 tablespoon cumin seeds

One 26-ounce jar Newman's Own Sockarooni Sauce

One 16-ounce jar Newman's Own Mild or Medium Salsa

1 1/2 cups water

1 cup dried figs or pitted prunes, halved

1 cup dried apricots, chopped

1/2 cup whole-berry cranberry sauce

One 3-inch-long cinnamon stick

One 24-ounce package cooked polenta, cut into 1/2-inch-thick slices

Fresh cilantro sprigs for garnish

✪ Preheat the oven to 300 degrees.

✪ Place the chiles on a baking sheet and bake for 5 minutes, until puffed; check to see that the chiles do not burn. Transfer the chiles to a bowl and cover with boiling water. Let stand for 20 minutes. Drain the chiles and puree in a blender.

✪ In a large locking plastic bag, combine the flour, mustard, coriander and pepper. Add the pork cubes, seal the bag well and shake until the pork is lightly coated.

✪ In a 6-quart Dutch oven, heat 2 tablespoons of the oil over medium-high heat. Add half of the pork cubes and sauté for about 10 minutes, until browned on all sides. Transfer the browned pork to a bowl; continue the browning process with the remaining oil and pork cubes.

✪ Return the pork to the Dutch oven. Add the brown sugar and cumin seeds and sauté for 1 minute. Add the Sockarooni sauce, salsa, water, figs or prunes, apricots and cranberry sauce and stir gently. Add the chile puree and cinnamon stick.

✪ Bring the mixture to a boil over high heat. Cover the pot, reduce the heat to low and simmer for about 1 hour and 30 minutes, until the pork is tender.

✪ About 20 minutes before serving, preheat the oven to 375 degrees and grease a large baking sheet. Arrange the polenta slices on the baking sheet. Bake the polenta for about 10 minutes, until hot.

✪ Serve the ragout over the polenta slices garnished with fresh cilantro sprigs.

SERVES 8

GREEK STUFFED BURGERS
WITH CUCUMBER-YOGURT SAUCE

Newman's Own / Good Housekeeping Recipe Contest

Finalist, 1998: Gigi Jensen Wychor, Shoreview, Minnesota • For a company dinner, Gigi decided to spice up her recipe for spinach and feta burgers with prepared balsamic salad dressing.

One 10-ounce package frozen chopped spinach, thawed and squeezed dry

4 ounces feta cheese, crumbled

4 ounces sliced ripe black olives

2 green onions, chopped

2 cloves garlic, minced

1 teaspoon dried oregano

³/₄ teaspoon freshly ground black pepper

¹/₂ cup Newman's Own Balsamic Vinaigrette Salad Dressing

1¹/₂ pounds lean ground beef

¹/₂ teaspoon salt

CUCUMBER-YOGURT SAUCE

¹/₂ cup plain low-fat yogurt

¹/₄ cup Newman's Own Balsamic Vinaigrette Salad Dressing

¹/₄ small cucumber, peeled and finely chopped (¹/₂ cup)

4 whole wheat hamburger buns

Lettuce leaves and tomato slices for garnish

✪ In a bowl, combine the spinach, feta cheese, olives, green onions, garlic, oregano, ¹/₂ teaspoon of the pepper and ¹/₂ cup salad dressing and mix with a fork until well blended.

✪ In a medium bowl, mix the beef with the salt and remaining ¹/₄ teaspoon pepper. Divide the beef mixture into 8 equal portions and shape each portion into a ³/₄-inch-thick patty.

✪ Place a heaping tablespoon of the spinach mixture in the center of each patty. Top with the remaining 4 patties and pinch the edges of the patties together to seal.

✪ Lightly spray a 12-inch nonstick skillet with olive oil cooking spray. Heat the skillet over medium heat.

✪ Place the patties in the skillet and cook for 6 to 8 minutes, or until the meat is cooked to desired doneness, turning halfway through the cooking time. Top the patties with the remaining spinach mixture, dividing evenly. Cover the skillet and cook for 3 minutes.

✪ For the cucumber-yogurt sauce, whisk the ingredients together in a bowl.

✪ Serve the patties on buns garnished with lettuce, tomato and cucumber-yogurt sauce.

SERVES 4

SOCKAROONI ORANGE KISS-ME CAKE

Newman's Own / Good Housekeeping Recipe Contest

*Reprinted from "Newman's Own Cookbook" (Simon and Schuster): Kim Landhuis,
Fort Dodge, Iowa • No one will ever guess the secret ingredient in this sweet and tangy cake,
which secured a 1997 runner-up prize in the recipe contest.*

2 large eggs

1 cup Newman's Own Sockarooni
   Spaghetti Sauce

3/4 cup freshly squeezed orange juice

1/2 cup vegetable oil

3 cups flour

1 1/2 cups sugar

2 teaspoons pumpkin pie spice

1 1/2 teaspoons baking powder

1 1/2 teaspoons baking soda

1 1/2 cups golden raisins

1 cup chopped almonds

FROSTING

6 ounces low-fat cream cheese, softened

2 tablespoons unsalted butter or
   margarine, softened

1/4 cup freshly squeezed orange juice

1/2 teaspoon freshly grated orange zest

1 pound confectioners' sugar

Dried cherries for garnish

Almond slices for garnish

✪ Preheat the oven to 350 degrees. Grease a 10-inch Bundt or tube pan.

✪ In a large bowl, beat the eggs. Add the spaghetti sauce, orange juice and oil and mix well.

✪ In another large bowl, combine the flour, sugar, pumpkin pie spice, baking powder and baking soda. Add the flour mixture to the egg mixture and beat slowly until mixed. Add the raisins and almonds and mix well.

✪ Pour the batter into the prepared pan and bake for 40 to 50 minutes, or until a toothpick inserted into the center of the cake comes out clean.

✪ Cool the cake on a rack for 15 minutes. Remove the cake from the pan and cool completely.

✪ For the frosting, combine the cream cheese, butter, orange juice and orange zest in a large bowl and beat until light and fluffy. Gradually add the confectioners' sugar, beating until the frosting is smooth.

✪ Spread the frosting on the cooled cake. Garnish the cake with dried cherries and sliced almonds.

✪ Cut the cake into wedges to serve.

SERVES 12

THE BARBECUE COMPANY Q-SAUCE

Best in the West Nugget Rib Cook-Off

Winner, Best Sauce: The Barbecue Company, Phoenix, Arizona · This recipe can be multiplied to make larger quantities, but it may need to simmer for a longer period of time. Extras can be stored in containers in the freezer, but make sure the sauce has cooled completely before freezing.

2 tablespoons vegetable oil

1³/₄ ounces chopped yellow onion

22 ounces ketchup

2¹/₂ ounces teriyaki sauce

1¹/₃ ounces honey

1¹/₄ ounces dark corn syrup

¹/₄ ounce red wine vinegar

³/₄ ounce Worcestershire sauce

³/₄ ounce Liquid Smoke

³/₄ ounce Dijon-style mustard

1³/₄ ounces brown sugar

1¹/₂ ounces cayenne pepper

¹/₂ teaspoon granulated garlic

¹/₂ teaspoon freshly ground black pepper

¹/₂ teaspoon celery seeds

✪ In a saucepan, heat the oil over medium-high heat. Add the onion and sauté until caramelized.

✪ Add the remaining ingredients and bring to a boil over high heat. Reduce the heat to low and simmer for 1 to 2 hours, stirring every 20 minutes.

✪ Cool before using.

MAKES 1 QUART

BACK FORTY TEXAS BARBECUE SAUCE

Best in the West Nugget Rib Cook-Off

People's Choice Award, Best Sauce: Back Forty Texas Barbecue, Pleasant Hill, California · Make this sauce when you're in the mood for a spicy accompaniment for ribs, chicken or other barbecued dishes.

1 cup ketchup

²/₃ cup Worcestershire sauce

²/₃ cup brown sugar

¹/₂ teaspoon hot pepper sauce

1 teaspoon cayenne pepper

1 teaspoon freshly ground black pepper

1 teaspoon salt

1 teaspoon paprika

1 teaspoon chili powder

2 tablespoons mustard

1 tablespoon Liquid Smoke

¹/₂ teaspoon crushed garlic

¹/₄ cup flour

1¹/₂ cups water

✪ In a large heavy pot, add the ingredients in the order listed.

✪ Place the pot over low heat and cook for 1 to 2 hours, stirring every 20 minutes, until thickened.

✪ Cool before using.

MAKES 1 QUART

Back Forty Texas Barbecue Dry Rub

Best in the West Nugget Rib Cook-Off

Back Forty Texas Barbecue, Pleasant Hill, California · A dry rub is a mixture of dried herbs and ground spices that are rubbed over the surface of meats, poultry or fish before grilling or smoking.

¼ cup freshly ground black pepper

1 tablespoon plus ½ teaspoon paprika

1 tablespoon salt

1 tablespoon garlic powder

½ tablespoon turmeric

Dash cayenne pepper

✪ In a bowl, mix all ingredients together thoroughly.

MAKES ½ CUP

BJ's Barbecued Beans

Best in the West Nugget Rib Cook-Off

Peter and Kelly Rathmann, BJ's Barbecue, Sparks, Nevada • For extra smoky flavor, place these beans on the grill grid over a charcoal fire while you are cooking the meat or poultry entrée.

One 1-pound bag dried pinto beans, soaked overnight in water to cover

½ cup packed brown sugar

1¼ cups barbecue sauce

2 tablespoons mustard

1 heaping tablespoon chili powder

✪ Drain the beans. Add the drained beans to a large saucepan and cover with fresh cold water. Bring the water just to a boil. Reduce the heat to low and simmer the beans until tender. Drain the beans well.

✪ Place the beans in a saucepan with the remaining ingredients and mix well. Heat over medium heat until the flavors are blended and the mixture is hot throughout.

SERVES 4 TO 6

PECAN PIE

Best in the West Nugget Rib Cook-Off

Back Forty Texas Barbecue, Pleasant Hill, California · The Back Forty crew believes that there are only two authentic desserts to end a barbecue meal — banana pudding and pecan pie. Here's their version of the pie.

4 eggs

2 tablespoons half-and-half

1½ cups light corn syrup

⅓ cup flour

⅓ cup sugar

1 teaspoon vanilla extract

2 tablespoons margarine, melted

One 9-inch pie pastry

1 cup pecan pieces

✪ Preheat the oven to 350 degrees.

✪ In a large bowl, beat the eggs. Add the half-and-half, corn syrup, flour, sugar, vanilla and margarine and mix well.

✪ Line a 9-inch pie pan with the pie pastry. Place the pecan pieces in the pan. Pour the egg mixture evenly over the pecans.

✪ Bake the pie for 1 hour. Cool and cut into wedges.

MAKES ONE 9-INCH PIE

GRILLED PORK LOIN WITH APPLE AND ZUCCHINI

Best in the West Nugget Rib Cook-Off

Courtesy of Chris Johnson, Executive Chef, Raincity Grill · Hearty appetites will be satisfied with this dish. The chili flakes add just the right amount of zip to the rich, slightly sweet sauce.

Six 10- to 12-ounce bone-in pork
  loin chops

1/4 cup minced shallots

2 tablespoons freshly ground pepper

4 tablespoons olive oil

3 medium-size green or yellow zucchini,
  peeled and cut in half lengthwise,
  and cut into 1/2-inch slices

1 small red onion, peeled and thinly sliced

3 Granny Smith apples, peeled,
  quartered, cored, and cut into 1/2-inch
  thick slices

2 tablespoons chili flakes

1/2 cup honey

3 cups apple juice

1 cup veal stock

18 small new potatoes, cooked
  and cooled

✪ Place the pork chops in a large shallow bowl.

✪ Mix the shallots, pepper, and 3 tablespoons of the olive oil together and rub evenly over the pork chops. Marinate in the refrigerator for 2 hours.

✪ Grill the pork chops over medium-hot fire for 5 to 6 minutes per side for medium doneness. Keep warm.

✪ On the side of the grill, cook the zucchini slices until tender and browned. Keep warm.

✪ While the pork is grilling, heat the remaining 1 tablespoon oil in a medium skillet and saute the onion and apples with the chili flakes until the apples are golden and the onions are limp. Add the honey and apple juice and cook until the mixture is reduced by one-third. Add the veal stock and cook until the mixture is reduced by one-third. Add the cooked potatoes to the sauce and cook until the potatoes are heated through.

✪ Place two pork chops on each serving plate. Spoon a generous amount of the sauce over the chops. Arrange the potatoes and grilled zucchini strips on each plate. Serve immediately.

SERVES 6

LEMON-SOUR CREAM CUSTARD PIE

National Pie Championships

First Place, Cream and Custard Category, Amateur Division: Curtis Maddox •
According to Curtis, a wedge of custard pie should be very high and generous on the plate.
Curtis's recipe makes two pies—one for eating and one for giving.

PASTRY

2 cups flour

1 generous teaspoon salt

2/3 cups vegetable shortening

5 to 6 tablespoons ice water

FILLING

6 eggs, separated

Grated zest and juice of 3 lemons

2 cups sugar

3/4 cup flour

1 cup milk

1 cup buttermilk

1 cup sour cream

3 tablespoons unsalted butter, melted

1 teaspoon vanilla extract

✪ For the pastry, mix the flour and salt in a shallow bowl. Add the shortening and, with a pastry blender or two knifes, cut it into the flour mixture until the mixture resembles small peas. Slowly add the ice water, tossing thoroughly with a fork until the mixture is just moistened.

✪ With lightly floured hands, toss the mixture from the bottom to the top until the ingredients are distributed, taking care not to squeeze the mixture. Gently form the dough into a ball and refrigerate for 20 to 30 minutes.

✪ Divide the dough into 2 pieces. On a lightly floured work surface, roll each dough piece into a 10- to 10½-inch circle. Carefully transfer the dough to two 9-inch pie pans.

✪ Lightly moisten the under-edge of the pastry and fold under to form a rim. (Fill the pie shells immediately, or freeze until ready to fill and bake.)

✪ Preheat the oven to 450 degrees.

✪ For the filling, place the egg yolks in a bowl and beat until light yellow in color. Add the lemon zest and mix well. While beating, slowly add the lemon juice.

✪ Add the sugar and flour and beat slowly until incorporated. Add the milk, buttermilk and sour cream and beat slowly until incorporated. Add the melted butter and vanilla and beat slowly until incorporated.

✪ In another bowl, beat the egg whites until stiff peaks form. Add the egg whites into the egg yolk mixture and fold until the ingredients are incorporated.

✪ Fill the prepared pastry shells with the filling, dividing evenly. Bake the pies for 15 minutes. Reduce the oven heat to 350 degrees and bake for 40 minutes; the top will caramelize slowly and rise high in the pan.

✪ Remove the pies from the oven and place on a wire rack to cool; the filling will shrink as the pies cool.

✪ Serve the pies slightly warm or at room temperature and cut into wedges.

MAKES TWO 9-INCH PIES

SOUTHERN EXPOSURE KEY LIME PIE

National Pie Championships

First Place, Cream Pie Category, Retail Division: Bruce Monette, Niwot, Colorado · Bruce developed this pie for his Southern-themed restaurant, Southern Exposure. Key limes are a special variety of limes that have a yellow-green color and unique flavor. Look for Key limes, which come from Florida, in a specialty food store. The juice also comes in bottles.

1/2 cup real Key lime juice (fresh or bottled)

5 large egg yolks

One 15-ounce can sweetened condensed milk

One prepared graham cracker crust

1 cup heavy cream, chilled (preferably not ultra-pasteurized)

1/4 cup sugar

1 teaspoon double-strength vanilla extract

Grated fresh lime zest for garnish

✪ Preheat the oven to 350 degrees.

✪ In a bowl, mix the Key lime juice, egg yolks and condensed milk with a wire whisk until blended. Pour the egg yolk mixture into the prepared crust.

✪ Bake the pie for 10 minutes. Remove the pie from the oven and cool to room temperature. Place in the refrigerator to chill.

✪ In a bowl, whip the cream with the sugar and vanilla until light and fluffy.

✪ Garnish the chilled pie with whipped cream and lime zest and refrigerate until serving time. Cut into wedges to serve.

MAKES ONE 9- TO 10-INCH PIE

RHUBARB-STRAWBERRY-RASPBERRY PIE

National Pie Championships

Best of Show, Amateur Division: Susan Gills • Susan deftly combines two types of berries and rhubarb in a sweet and tangy filling for a summertime pie.

FILLING

3/4 cup sugar

1/3 cup flour

1 cup fresh strawberry halves or quarters

1 cup fresh raspberries

2 cups rhubarb pieces, 1/2-inch pieces

PASTRY

2 cups flour

1 teaspoon salt

2/3 cup vegetable shortening

2 tablespoons butter

4 tablespoons ice-cold water

1 tablespoon butter, melted

1 teaspoon lemon juice

Sugar

✪ For the filling, mix the sugar and flour in a bowl. Add the strawberries, raspberries and rhubarb and mix well. Cover the bowl and refrigerate overnight.

✪ For the pastry, mix the flour and salt in a shallow bowl. Add the shortening and butter. With a pastry blender or 2 knives, cut the mixture until it resembles coarse cornmeal.

✪ Slowly add the water and toss the ingredients together until incorporated.

✪ With your hands, gently form the dough into a ball. Wrap the dough with plastic wrap and refrigerate for at least 20 minutes.

✪ Preheat the oven to 400 degrees.

✪ Divide the dough in half. On a lightly floured work surface, roll out one half of the dough to a 10-inch circle. Carefully transfer the dough to a 9-inch pie pan.

✪ Pour the berry mixture into the pan and drizzle with the melted butter and lemon juice.

✪ On a lightly floured work surface, roll out the remaining half of the dough to a 9 1/2-inch circle. Carefully transfer the dough on the top of the filling. Fold over the edges of the bottom pastry over the top pastry and crimp the edges. Sprinkle the top of the pie lightly with sugar. With a knife, very carefully cut a few steam vents into the top of the pie.

✪ Bake the pie for 10 minutes. Reduce the oven heat to 350 degrees and bake the pie for 40 to 50 minutes longer, until the crust is golden brown.

✪ Cool the pie completely before cutting into wedges to serve.

SERVES 8 TO 10

Pumpkin Butternut Squash Soup

Half Moon Bay Art and Pumpkin Festival

Ed Chamberlain, Chef, Lowell Inn, Stillwater, Minnesota · Ed's recipe boasts two types of winter squash: pumpkin and butternut. Serving his soup in miniature pumpkin shells is perfect for a fall season dinner party.

4 miniature (baking) pumpkins (optional)

2 medium butternut squash

4 cups chicken stock

2 cups fresh or canned pumpkin puree

$1/2$ cup honey

1 tablespoon chopped fresh ginger

1 teaspoon ground cardamom

$1/4$ teaspoon ground allspice

Salt and freshly ground pepper to taste

2 cups heavy cream

Crème fraîche flavored with minced fresh ginger for garnish

Croutons for garnish

✪ Heat the oven to 350 degrees.

✪ Remove the tops from the miniature pumpkins, if using, and scoop out the seeds. Place on a foil-lined baking sheet and bake for about 50 minutes, until tender.

✪ With a sturdy vegetable peeler, peel the squash and cut into chunks. Place the squash chunks in a saucepan with the chicken stock and bring to a boil over high heat. Reduce the heat to low and simmer until tender. Transfer the squash and some of the stock to a food processor and puree until smooth.

✪ Return the squash puree to the pot with the stock. Add the pumpkin puree, honey, ginger, cardamom, allspice, salt and pepper and heat, stirring, until smooth and heated through. Add the heavy cream and stir until blended.

✪ Serve the soup in the mini pumpkin shells or in soup bowls. Garnish with crème fraîche and croutons.

SERVES 4

PUMPKIN RISOTTO

Half Moon Bay Art and Pumpkin Festival

Michelle McRaney, Chef, Mr. B's Bistro, New Orleans, Louisiana • Serve Michelle's hearty risotto as an entrée accompanied by a tossed green salad and bread. Or, serve it as a side dish for roasted meat or poultry.

5 cups chicken stock

2 tablespoons butter

1 medium onion, diced small

1 pound Arborio rice

1 cup dry white wine

1 cup roasted pumpkin, mashed

4 ounces applewood-smoked bacon, cooked and crumbled

3 tablespoons freshly grated Parmesan cheese

Salt and freshly ground black pepper to taste

Toasted pumpkin seeds for garnish

✪ In a saucepan, bring the chicken stock to a boil over high heat. Reduce the heat to low and keep the stock at a simmer.

✪ In a heavy saucepan, heat the butter over medium-high heat. Add the onion and sauté until softened, about 3 minutes. Add the rice and stir to coat the rice grains with butter.

✪ Add the wine and cook, stirring, until the wine is almost evaporated. Add 1 cup of the simmering chicken stock and cook, stirring constantly, until the liquid is almost all absorbed.

✪ Add another cup of the chicken stock and cook, stirring constantly, until the liquid is almost all absorbed. Continue the cooking process until you have added almost all of the stock and the rice is nearly cooked, but still has a small hard center.

✪ Reduce the heat to low and stir in the pumpkin, bacon and Parmesan. Adjust the seasonings with salt and pepper.

✪ Garnish servings with toasted pumpkin seeds.

SERVES 4

WORLD-FAMOUS PUMPKIN ROLLS

Half Moon Bay Art and Pumpkin Festival

Courtesy of the Half Moon Bay 4-H Club · The combination of pumpkin and spices in this dessert creates a flavor similar to gingerbread.

3 eggs

1 cup granulated sugar

²/₃ cups pumpkin puree

1 teaspoon lemon juice

³/₄ cup flour

1 teaspoon baking powder

2 teaspoons ground cinnamon

1 teaspoon ground ginger

¹/₂ teaspoon ground nutmeg

¹/₂ teaspoon salt

¹/₂ cup finely chopped walnuts

Confectioners' sugar

FILLING

1 cup confectioners' sugar

¹/₄ cup butter, at room temperature

Two 3-ounce packages cream cheese, at room temperature

¹/₂ teaspoon vanilla extract

✪ Preheat the oven to 375 degrees. Grease and flour a 15-x-10-x-1-inch jelly roll pan.

✪ With an electric mixer, beat the eggs on high speed for 5 minutes. While beating, gradually add the granulated sugar. Stir in the pumpkin puree and lemon juice.

✪ In a bowl, sift together the flour, baking powder, cinnamon, ginger, nutmeg and salt.

✪ With a rubber spatula, fold the flour mixture into the pumpkin mixture. Spread the batter evenly into the prepared pan, smoothing the top with the spatula.

✪ Sprinkle the batter with the finely chopped walnuts and bake for 15 minutes.

✪ Place a clean dishtowel on a work surface and sprinkle with a moderate amount of confectioners' sugar. Carefully invert the cake onto the towel. Starting at the narrow end, roll the cake in the towel jelly roll-style. Cool the cake completely.

✪ For the filling, combine the confectioners' sugar, butter, cream cheese and vanilla in a bowl. With an electric mixer, beat the ingredients until smooth.

✪ Unroll the cake and spread evenly with the filling. Roll the cake and the filling, without the towel, jelly roll-style. Wrap the filled cake with plastic wrap and chill completely.

✪ To serve, remove the plastic wrap and carefully cut the cake into 1-inch-wide slices.

SERVES 10

PUMPKIN CHEESECAKE

Half Moon Bay Art and Pumpkin Festival

*Reprinted from the Coastal Harvest Cookbook (Main Street Beautification Committee):
Kris Mason and Jo Ann Wherry • Your guests will think you labored long and hard when they
taste this cheesecake. But it's really not hard to make, and you can make it ahead of time.
The secret to a perfectly textured cheesecake lies in the baking technique.*

CRUST

1 cup pecans (about 4 ounces), chopped

1 cup graham cracker crumbs

2 tablespoons sugar

5 tablespoons unsalted butter, melted

FILLING

2½ pounds cream cheese, at room temperature

1 cup sugar

4 large eggs, lightly beaten

3 egg yolks, lightly beaten

3 tablespoons flour

2 teaspoons ground cinnamon

1 teaspoon ground cloves

1 teaspoon ground ginger

1 cup heavy cream

1 tablespoon vanilla extract

16 ounces pumpkin puree

Whipped cream for garnish

✪ Preheat the oven to 350 degrees.

✪ For the crust, mix together the pecans, graham cracker crumbs and sugar. Make a well in the center and add the melted butter. Mix with a fork or your fingers until blended.

✪ Press the crust into the bottom and about 1-inch up the sides of a 10-inch springform pan.

✪ For the filling, combine the cream cheese, sugar, eggs and egg yolks in a large mixing bowl. With an electric mixer, mix the ingredients until blended.

✪ Add the flour, cinnamon, cloves and ginger and beat until mixed. Beat in the cream and vanilla.

✪ Add the pumpkin puree and beat on medium speed until well mixed.

✪ Pour the filling mixture into the springform pan and bake for 15 minutes.

✪ Reduce the oven heat to 275 degrees and bake for 1 hour. Turn off the oven heat and leave the cake in the oven for 2 hours.

✪ Cover the cheesecake and chill until ready to serve. Serve garnished with whipped cream.

SERVES 8

CREAM OF VIDALIA ONION SOUP

Vidalia Onion Festival

First Place, Professional Category: Ruth M. Underwood, Vidalia, Georgia · Vidalias are an ultra-sweet onion variety grown in the town of Vidalia, Georgia. They have a short season, which occurs in spring and early summer. If you see them in your local store, snap up a bunch to use in recipes.

³/₄ cup butter

3 cups sliced Vidalia onions

¹/₄ cup all-purpose flour

1 teaspoon salt

¹/₂ teaspoon freshly ground black pepper

2¹/₂ cups milk

1¹/₂ cups half-and-half

Shredded cheese to taste, of your choice

Chopped fresh parsley for garnish

✪ In a skillet, melt ¹/₂ cup of the butter over medium heat. Add the onions and sauté until tender; set aside.

✪ In a Dutch oven, melt the remaining ¹/₄ cup butter over medium-low heat. Add the flour, salt and pepper and stir until smooth. Cook for 1 minute.

✪ Gradually add the milk and half-and-half and cook over medium heat, stirring constantly, until thickened.

✪ Stir in the onions and reduce the heat to low. Simmer for a few minutes to blend the flavors.

✪ Add the cheese to taste.

✪ Garnish servings with chopped parsley.

SERVES 6 TO 8

YUMMY SAUSAGE BUNDLES

Vidalia Onion Festival

Overall Winner: Rebekah Arnold, Vidalia, Georgia • Rebekah buys two tubes of biscuits for this recipe: one 8-count tube and one 5-count tube. She bakes the leftover biscuit on a piece a foil for eating separately while assembling the recipe.

½ pound bulk sausage

½ cup finely chopped Vidalia onion

½ cup chopped mushrooms

¾ cup grated sharp cheddar cheese

¾ teaspoon prepared mustard

¾ teaspoon Worcestershire sauce

¼ cup milk

12 big flaky biscuits from a tube

1 egg white, beaten

✪ Preheat the oven to 375 degrees. Spray a 12-cup muffin pan with nonstick cooking spray.

✪ In a skillet, cook the sausage over medium-high heat, crumbling with a fork, until the sausage is browned and no pink remains. With a slotted spoon, transfer the sausage to a colander to drain.

✪ Remove and discard all but 1 tablespoon of the sausage fat from the skillet. Add the onion and mushrooms to the skillet and sauté until softened. Transfer the mixture to a bowl with the drained sausage and mix well.

✪ In another bowl, combine the cheese, mustard, Worcestershire and milk and mix well. Add the cheese mixture to the sausage mixture and mix well.

✪ Separate the biscuits and place on a work surface. Peel 2 layers of dough from each biscuit and set aside. With your fingers, flatten the remaining portions of biscuit dough and use the portions to line the muffin cups, forming 12 "crusts."

✪ Divide the sausage filling evenly among the crusts. Place the remaining biscuit dough portions on top of the sausage filling, pressing the crusts together and pinching them around the sides to seal the filling.

✪ Brush the tops of the bundles with beaten egg white. Bake the bundles for 12 to 15 minutes, or until golden brown. Cool on a rack.

MAKES 12 BUNDLES

SAVORY APPLE ONION BREAD

Vidalia Onion Festival

Mary Woodruff, Vidalia, Georgia · If you can't find hot roll mix, you can use 1 pound of self-rising flour mixed with 1 teaspoon salt and 1 package instant yeast.

1 tablespoon butter

1 Golden Delicious apple

1/2 cup chopped Vidalia onion

One 16-ounce package hot roll mix

1 cup shredded cheddar cheese

2 tablespoons chopped red bell pepper

1 tablespoon caraway seeds

1 egg, slightly beaten

1 cup hot water

✪ In a small skillet, heat the butter over medium heat. Add the apple and onion and sauté until tender; set aside.

✪ In a large bowl, combine the hot roll mix, cheese, red pepper and caraway seeds and mix well. Add the egg, water and apple-onion mixture and mix well with a wooden spoon. Stir until the dough pulls away from the sides of the bowl.

✪ Transfer the dough to a lightly floured work surface and knead with your hands for 5 minutes.

✪ Return the dough to the mixing bowl, cover with plastic wrap and let the dough rest for 5 minutes.

✪ Grease a 1 1/2-quart baking dish or a loaf pan. Place the dough in the dish, cover and let rise for 30 minutes.

✪ Preheat the oven to 375 degrees.

✪ Bake the bread for 30 to 35 minutes, until it sounds hollow when thumped.

MAKES 1 LOAF

Cook-Off America kitchen courtesy of Wood-Mode

NOTES

INDEX

Index

INDEX

PERMISSIONS

The following recipes are courtesy of:

The American Pie Council: Lemon-Sour Cream Custard Pie; Rhubarb-Strawberry-Raspberry Pie; Southern Exposure Key Lime Pie

The Catfish Institute: Cashew-Crusted Catfish with Tomato-Basil Cream; Catfish Stuffed with Basil-Olive Pesto; Catfish Wrap with Gado Gado Sauce

Ed Chamberlain: Pumpkin Butternut Squash Soup

David Corley and James Crocker: Apple Coleslaw

Epicure Catering, Ventura, California: Chicken Picatta

Jeff Erb: Back Forty Texas BBQ Sauce; Back Forty Texas BBQ Dry Rub; Pecan Pie

The Fat Boys' Barbecue Team: Barbecue Brisket; Caramel-Pecan Cheesecake

The Georgia Apple Festival: Cream Cheese Apple Pie; Miss Lo's Holiday Apple Cake

The Gilroy Garlic Festival Association: Baked Stuffed Portobello Mushroom Caps; Garlic Spring Rolls with Garlicky Lime Sauce; Flamboyant Flank Steak with Fragrant Filling

The Gonzales Jambalaya Festival: Chicken Jambalaya

Half Moon Bay 4-H Club: World Famous Pumpkin Rolls

The Henry Ford Museum & Greenfield Village: Dutch-Style Pea Soup; Gingerbread Cake; Potato Pudding; Sauerkraut Dressing for Poultry

The Heritage Salmon Company: Grilled Citrus Salmon; Grilled Salmon with Mustard and Dill; Simple Grilled Salmon

The Hi-Tech Smokers Barbecue Team: Barbecued Beans; Grilled Barbecue-Spiced Potatoes; Sautéed Vegetables

The International Chili Society: 24-Karat Chili; B&M's Double-Flush Salsa; Gold Miner's Chili; Stoney Road Tomato Salsa

Andrew Jepsen: The Barbecue Company Q-Sauce

Chris Johnson: Grilled Pork Loin with Apple and Zucchini

Land O'Lakes, Inc.: Raspberry Walnut Shortbread Bars

Michael Latuso, Sr.: Simmered White Beans

Vickie Mahan: Lemon Meringue Pie

Michelle McRaney: Pumpkin Risotto

Maine Department of Aqua Resources: Grilled Salmon in Tequila-Lime Marinade with Tropical Fruit Salsa and Caribbean Wild Rice; Maple-Glazed Atlantic Salmon Fillets with Apples, Grilled Potatoes and Baby Carrots

Mama Mary's Gourmet Pizza Crusts Pizza Creations Contest: Apple Streusel Dessert Pizza; Berry Crunchy Dessert Pizza; Sizzlin' Spicy Scampi Pizza; Smoky Three-Cheese White Pizza

The Massachusetts Cranberry Harvest Festival: Cranberry Balsamic Chicken with Portobellos, Rice Pilaf and Spiced Sweet Potatoes; Cranberry Pineapple Torte

The Mudcreek BBQ & Chili Co.: Grilled Bratwurst

The Mushroom Festival: Easy Mushroom Brunch Bake; Herb-Stuffed Chicken Breasts; Marinated Duck Breasts with Exotic Mushroom Timbale, Spaghetti Squash and Fall Fruit Compote; Mushroom Napoleon; Resplendent Stuffed Mushrooms; Vegetable Risotto Cakes with Mushrooms

Newman's Own/Good Housekeeping Recipe Contest: Greek Stuffed Burgers with Cucumber-Yogurt Sauce; Rally 'Round the Ragout, Boys!; Vermont Fiesta Paulkets

North American Olive Oil Association: Fork-Tender Stuffed Pork Roast; Mediterranean Chocolate Cake; Onion-Parmesan Focaccia; Roasted Red Pepper-Sun-Dried Tomato Spread

Jett Peterson: Smoked Salmon Frittata

Peter C. Rathmann: BJ's Barbecued Beans

Jake Southworth: Chocolate Chip Pecan Bread Pudding with Whiskey Cream

St. Mary's County Oyster Festival: Oyster Cheesecakes with Oyster Sauce and Caviar; Oyster 'n Fennel Chowder; Sicilian Oyster Salad

Sutter Home Winery: Caesar Salad & Flank Steak Burgers on Garlic Crostini; Caribbean Couscous Burgers; Carolina Pork Barbecue Burgers; Stilton and Toasted Walnut Burgers with Grilled Tomatoes and Spicy Leeks

The Three Little Pigs BBQ Team: Three Little Pigs Pork Butt

The US Apple Association: French-Style Chicken with Apples

The USA Smoke Barbecue Team: Barbecued Texas Brisket; Grilled Chicken

Vidalia Tourism Council: Cream of Vidalia Onion Soup; Savory Apple-Onion Bread; Yummy Sausage Bundles

The following recipes are courtesy of the author or publisher:

From *Citrus* by Ethel and Georgeanne Brennan (Chronicle Books): Lemon Butter Cookies; Potato Soup with Meyer Lemons

From *The Coastal Harvest Cookbook* by Kris Mason and Jo Ann Wherry: Pumpkin Cheesecake

From *Jack Daniel's The Spirit of Tennessee Cookbook* by Lynne Tolley and Pat Mitchamore (Rutledge Hill Press, Nashville, Tennessee): Onion and Apple Bake; Corn Light Bread; Southern Greens with Pot Liquor

From *John Willingham's World Champion Bar-B-Q* by John Willingham (William Morrow and Company): Bar-B-Q'd Pork Pizza

From *The Kansas City Barbecue Society Cookbook*: Grilled Cheese Potatoes; Old Country Potato Salad

From *The Memphis in May International Festival Cookbook*: Chocolate Praline Jumbo Mud Squares; Holy Smoker's Red Beans & Rice; Hot Cabbage Slaw; Land O' Cotton Hawg Cookers' Pork Ribs; Super Swine Sizzlers' Pork Shoulder

From *Newman's Own Cookbook* by Paul Newman and A.E. Hotchner (Simon & Schuster): Sockarooni Orange Kiss-Me Cake

From *Old World Swiss Family Recipes*: Roesti; Kaesekuchen; Swiss Cheese Fondue

From *The St. Teresa of Avila School Cookbook*: Sweet Potato Casserole

From *Wisconsin Food Festivals* by Terese Allan: Cheese Days Deep-Fried Cheese Curds

Acknowledgements

Cook-Off America was a large, ambitious project, which required a great deal of support, patience, and expertise. We are very fortunate to have secured so many people and companies who were willing to get behind the project and turn it into a success.

The Weber-Stephen Products Company was the first company to come on board. Weber, which first invented the kettle grill in the 50's, is a visionary company whose products have given millions of people the gift of outdoor cooking. We are honored to have their support on this project. We are especially grateful to Mike Kempster, Sr. for his countless contributions and support. He has been a great guide and inspiration to us in the making of this series.

We are delighted to have the support of Colavita whose olive oil is a godsend to so many cooks, who use it for its tremendous flavor and health benefits. We are very grateful for their sponsorship and want to thank John Profaci, Jr., Lisa Gwirtzman and the others at Colavita.

We also grateful to Celebrity Cruises, who truly understand the meaning of a culinary journey, like Cook-Off America, which they prove by offering the finest cuisine in the cruise line industry (thanks to their superb chef, Michel Roux). Our special thanks go to Helen Burford and Mel Roth for their ongoing support and assistance.

Just as good wine enhances any good meal, Glen Ellen's sponsorship has been an enormous support to our series. We'd like to give a special toast to Priscilla Felton and Anne Howle of UDV who made this possible.

We also want to thank our talented an effervescent hosts, Narsai David and Mara Reid Rogers, who worked so diligently during the taping of the programs and did such a tremendous job presenting the recipes. They are both thoroughly professional and a delight to work with.

The exquisite kitchen set of Cook-Off America was provided by Wood-Mode, manufacturers of kitchen cabinetry. The brainchild of Bill Tobin and his team, the Cook-Off America set reflects the kind of beauty and unbeatable quality that Wood-Mode is known for.

Our appliances were courtesy of another top-of-the-line name, KitchenAid, who graciously provided us with both large and small kitchen appliances. Our thanks to Brian Maynard for all his tremendous efforts and his ongoing support of our projects.

Catherine Fischer of All-Clad Cookware also made sure that we were working with nothing but the best. It's easy to understand why All-Clad cookware is a favorite of so many professional chefs and home cooks.

Finally, we are blessed with the most hard-working, dedicated and talented production staff imaginable who made the entire experience of putting this show together a true delight: Vené Franco, Associate Producer, Eric Belanger and Gordon Winiemko, our editors, Bill Morris and Mike Varga, our lead cameramen, Kevan Brown, our field cameraman, and last but not least, the indefatigable, tireless and wonderful team of Dave Swanston and Rhonda Blewitt who take care of everything.
—Marjorie Poore and Alec Fatalevich

★

Cook-Off America ©1999 by Marjorie Poore Productions
Food photography: Darla Furlani
Location photography: Alec Fatalevich
Design: Kari Perin, Perin + Perin
Editing: Jennifer Newens
Production: Kristen Wurz
Research: Vené Franco

ISBN 0-9651095-4-2
Printed in Hong Kong through Global Interprint, Santa Rosa, California

10 9 8 7 6 5 4 3 2 1

MPP Books, 363 14th Avenue, San Francisco, CA 94118
Distributed by Bristol Publishing Enterprises, Inc.